Baby Momma Bliss

Breakthrough Success for Single Mothers

By

Baby Momma Bliss

Breakthrough Success for Single Mothers

By

Copyright © 2015 by Tanya Talley
All rights reserved. Published in the United States of America. Library of Congress Control Number: 2015907609

Copyright © 2015 Tanya Talley
This book may not be reproduced or transmitted in any form or by any means, graphic, electronic or mechanical, including photocopying, recording, taping or by any information storage or retrieval system, without the permission in writing from the Author.
This edition published by Creating Bliss Publishing. For information address Tanya Talley via tanyatalley.com
ISBN 978-0-692-34429-3
Baby Momma Bliss is a trademark of Tanya Talley.
B.L.I.S.S. is a trademark of Tanya Talley
Library of Congress Control Number: 2015907609

Talley, Tanya, 2015-
Baby Momma Bliss. — First edition.
Summary: "Breakthrough Success Facilitator, Tanya Talley shares her transformational personal development tools for single mothers. **B.L.I.S.S.** = **B**reakthrough **L**oving **I**nner **S**elf **S**uccess. Single mothers are encouraged to overcome negative situations and emotions in order to create a blissful life."
ISBN 978-0-69234-429-3
1. Single Mothers 2. Self-help 3. Anger Management 4. Parenting 1. Title.
Interior and exterior book design and production by Tanya Talley

For: Helen "Sister" Carr
     Layla and
     E. Sun
Perfect Love[3]

Introduction

Are you experiencing pain or struggle as a single mother? Many women do. There is hope. You can connect with your own inner bliss and live in single mother success. It's time to break out of baby momma and breakthrough to baby momma bliss. Baby momma bliss is single mother success.

Baby Momma?

What do people think when they hear baby momma? What do people mean when they say baby momma?

For the answer I turn to online user updated reference sites. Wikipedia.org, The Free Encyclopedia, says that *"A baby mama (also baby-mama and baby-mother) is a mother who is not married to her child's father, although the term is often infused with other meanings as well."*

So what are the other meanings? Urbandictionary.com is a reliable source for user updated definitions of colloquialisms.

A Baby mama is defined as *"Some chick you knocked up on accident during a fling who you can't stand but you have to tolerate cuz she got your **baby** now."* on urbandictionary.com.

Baby momma also carries a stigma because of the connection to the phrase baby momma drama. Baby momma drama refers to the problems that the man encounters while dealing with what his child's mother.

Tabloid magazines and news reporters are beginning to call single wealthy celebrities baby mommas but this is most likely used with the current "ironic" humor style. They are most likely thinking about how funny and ironic it was to call Angelina Jolie Brad Pitt's baby momma before they got married.

Baby Momma is a term that has many negative stereotypes. It started out as an urban ghetto term, but now it can be used for any single mother.

Baby Momma implies that something is missing. A *baby momma* situation means that a single mother has a child and no partner. Often there's some "Baby Momma Drama" in the situation as well.

If you are a single mother, dealing with a baby momma situation in your life, you may have to deal with a lot of complications in your life.

Do you have any problems that you would like to remove? Put an X in the box next any of the following problems that you are dealing with now:
- ☐ Family issues
- ☐ Anger issues
- ☐ Legal issues
- ☐ Money problems
- ☐ Codependent (energy draining) relationships
- ☐ An inner critic (negative thoughts about you or the things that you do)
- ☐ A need for more support/help
- ☐ A Dead end job
- ☐ Lack of education
- ☐ Self-destructive behavior
- ☐ Confusion about what to do next

Any of the situations above can get in the way of you reaching your goals. If you have any of these problems, you can fix them starting today. In the chapters that follow I will share how to fix these situations. This book will be your companion during your journey from *Baby Momma* drama to Single mom success.

If you have found yourself in a baby momma situation and you are dealing with the issues that can come with it; you can overcome every obstacle and reach your goals as a successful single mom.

In this book you will discover the key steps to single mom success without suffering.

If you are like most of my clients you probably want to do at least one of the following:
- Find out exactly what you want
- Finally *"make it"* and feel successful
- Overcome pain from your past
- Make more money
- Find your true love
- Change or improve your career
- Know that you are being a great mother.
- Break any cycle of negativity in your life

Sharing Solutions

Today my greatest joy is sharing this information with you.

Over the years I have learned that the answers come from inside. Imagine right now that everything that you need to build your life into anything that you want it to be is with you right now.

The first step is to have **B**reakthrough **L**oving **I**nner **S**elf **S**uccess and to find your B.L.I.S.S. Loving your inner self is connecting with the real you inside and your success.

In a baby momma situation there are many things to focus on that are outside of you. You focus on:
- Your child
- Your child's father
- Your own parents
- Your job
- People (at the school, at church, in your neighborhood, on the news etc.)

You worry about:
- The future
- The past
- What other people will do

With all of this going on, how can you ever connect with your own inner peace and success?
We have to make connecting with our inner peace, joy and purpose a habit.
This isn't complicated. It just takes practice.
Taking time to focus on you and what you are doing will cause you to breakthrough a baby momma situation. With focus on what you want, you can do anything that you can conceive in your mind.

When we were expecting our child, we may have thought that we had a partner. We may have thought that raising this man's child would be a partnership. When they called us baby momma, we may have been blindsided.

A shocking betrayal hurts. What's worse is that he may be betraying your child. Nothing can trigger more anger more quickly that hurting a mother's child.
 Some women have taken this turn of events to trigger a change in their attitude. Since the child's father hurt them, they turn angry. Since their relationship turned hopeless, they lost hope. Some even gave up on their joy. Some women decided only to live for their child.

I know what it feels like to go through all of it. I have been angry. I have wondered how I could ever make it. I tried living for my daughter but I soon realized that she and I deserved better lives than that. I didn't want my daughter to grow up with a zombie mommy who was half dead and only living for her. I knew that my daughter would be sad if I wasn't fully enjoying my life. I decided that finding my bliss was necessary. I had to find my bliss. Every mother needs her bliss to live her life to its fullest. Every mother has to live a blissful life to break the cycle of negativity.

Bliss means complete happiness or spiritual joy.
BLISS: Breakthrough Loving Inner Self Success.
B.L.I.S.S. comes from inside. It is with you right now.

None of our lives are perfect, but, we can have happiness and joy more often than not.

Once you have found bliss, you have the stability to do anything that you can imagine.

This book will help you to remove the issues around single motherhood and set you on your path to true B.L.I.S.S. from the inside and fulfilling the true purpose of your life.

My Story

My daughter Destiny and I were staying with a friend in a one bedroom apartment. Destiny and I slept on the futon in the living room.
My friend was accommodating and very understanding. However I was anxious. I had always been the independent type.
This particular night I was particularly anxious. I knew that I was at a crossroad in my life. It was one of those nights were I could no longer put off some important decisions.
I was facing a situation that had begun 36 months earlier. Back then I had a boyfriend who was caring and family oriented. We had been in a relationship for over six years. I attended all of his family functions with him. His father even told us that he wanted a grandchild from us. My boyfriend began to ask me many times to have his child.
I was the happiest that I had ever been in my life. I was nearing graduation from college. I was taking up to six aerobics workout classes per week. I finally felt healthy emotionally, mentally and physically.

I decided to have a child with him. I had no idea that I would break up with him by the time I was five months pregnant. It seemed like once I was pregnant we both changed in different directions. I was focused on getting ready for the baby and he seemed to spend a lot more time out drinking with his friends. I resented the changes that I saw in him.
We argued too much. It reminded me of the way that my parents would argue constantly. They were teenagers when I was born and throughout my time with them I wished that they would just break up. I didn't want my baby to listen to us arguing the way I had listened to my parents.
I decided that it was better for us to break up than to argue and fight while I was pregnant.
I thought that even though we had broken up, he would still be there for his daughter. When I had our baby girl, Destiny, I heard from him less and less. I believe that he loved our daughter but he didn't seem interested in her day to day life.
I had no choice. I had to pay attention to everything about Destiny. I didn't have much help from anyone so I had to make sure that our daughter had everything that she needed.
When Destiny reached one and a half year old, I took her to be evaluated because she wasn't saying clear words. Destiny was diagnosed with autism.

I was not prepared for my daughter to have special needs. The doctor told me to mourn the death of the child that I thought that I had. She stressed that little was known is about autism and there was no cure. This doctor told me that it was very likely that Destiny would never speak.

I was overwhelmed. I spent a couple sad days in the bed. Once I got up, I began working to help my Destiny. My hands were extremely full. I was coordinating Destiny's education. I was coordinating her therapy. I was constantly searching for the cure to autism. . Sometimes I felt like I was going to pass out because I was so stressed out and tired. I still couldn't stop because I didn't want Destiny to miss any treatments that could help her improve.

I couldn't accept that Destiny's father wasn't going to help. He knew that our daughter had autism but he still wasn't helping me with her care.

In the midst of all of this, I needed to move to a safer neighborhood and I was between apartments. My car's transmission went out. The bus drivers in my city went on strike so there was no bus to catch. There were historic wildfires burning in my city and I was allergic to the smoke.

I had been reaching out to Destiny's father to no avail. I felt confused. I knew that he had to love Destiny. I couldn't understand why he was becoming an absent father.
I thought that maybe if I explained my situation he would understand my fatigue and begin to help for Destiny's sake.

On that night, after my friend and Destiny had fallen asleep, I sat on the secluded back patio and I called Destiny's father. I was so nervous that I was shaking.

I wasn't going to talk at him or complain. I just wanted to be honest and garner his support for Destiny. When he answered immediately I felt hopeful. There was something in his voice that was much calmer than usual. I got the feeling that he had needed to receive this call just as much as I had needed to make the call.

After we exchanged hellos and a few pleasantries I got right to business. I said, *"...Our daughter is beautiful and I love her so much. She is my joy, but I get so tired every day. Every day I am exhausted from beginning to end. I am judged and criticized everyday by teachers, therapists, social workers and even strangers on the street. They see me struggling with her behaviors from the autism.*

This isn't easy. I have to fight to find services for her and to get her into programs. My worst fear is that I am not doing the best possible job.

All the while, I get nothing from you, nothing at all. It would be nice if you would help a little. Just do what you can.

You have a Liberal Arts degree to be an Elementary School teacher. Call the school for me. Maybe you could use your education and teaching credential to help. We could home school her to make sure that she is getting the best education available.

I don't know what to do. I don't know why I am so overwhelmed. I don't know how much longer I can continue like this…Can you help me in any way."

I was tired of the lies and excuses. I was ready to hear the truth. I think that his answer was honest and from the heart. That is why it hurt me so much.

 I believe that what he said was his truth and true to what I was living.
He paused briefly and then he said, "Tanya, You are my **baby momma**. That is what you are supposed to do. You are supposed to suffer and work hard and be there. I am not the mother, you are and you should have known that. I can't help you be a mother"

I was speechless. I felt a heavy pressure on my chest. I sat down and thought about what he said.

He had basically said that I was suffering because, as a mother, suffering was my job. He was right because that is what I had been doing.

I sat there holding the phone and both of us were silent. I said, "OK." and we both said goodbye and hung up.

I remembered the day that I brought our child to his apartment and he told his friend on the phone "My baby momma is over here and I'm about to babysit."

His remark had struck me with two red flags.
#1 Before I'd had the baby I was referred to as Tanya, a family member. What had happened to me being Tanya? Everyone knew me.

#2 How could he babysit his own child? Why didn't he say that he was spending time with Destiny?

His answer to my plea for help had given me the reason for the red flags. He revealed that he had asked me to have his child so that he could have a baby momma.

Looking back, all of his friends had baby mommas so of course he wanted one too.

All of his friend's baby momma's were suffering. They had to chase them around to get money. They were scrutinized.

I didn't think that my relationship would lead to a baby momma situation for me because we'd had a peaceful loving relationship.

Once I had gotten pregnant, things changed. By my fifth month, I was living in a domestic violence shelter.

Now He had his baby momma and it was me. I was his suffering baby momma.

I know that a lot of people believe that being a mother is about suffering but I didn't. Of course the job isn't easy but is doesn't have to be miserable. I didn't want my daughter to have a miserable mother.

I never expected that he would be an absent father. I never imagined that I would be called a baby momma. My parents were married and still together. I assumed that my daughter's biological father and I would stay together too. I felt ashamed of my situation.

I needed help with my daughter. I needed positive people to support me emotionally. I needed a career that could work for me. I needed financial freedom. I needed to forgive myself for getting into the situation. I needed to let go of my anger so that I could let love in again. I had to find my happiness because I didn't want my daughter to have an angry, sad or lonely mother. I remembered how much it hurt me when my mother wasn't happy. I wanted to do better for my daughter.

The good news is that I was able to focus and achieve my goals.

My number one goal became seeking my own joy. Why seek my own joy? Because:

- I wanted my daughter to have a happy mother.
- If I remained unhappy, Destiny's dad would use that as an excuse for his absence.
- I began to suspect that Destiny's dad was wishing me misery.
- The purpose of my life is to overcome adversity and find my joy.
- . I had overcome so many painful situations in my life. I knew that God hadn't saved me from all of my suffering in the past to have me suffer as a mother.

I gained my joy by giving it away.

I reclaimed my smile. I began volunteer work. I found mentors. I took feedback from others. I decided to remove as much negativity from my life as possible, including my own attitude, TV etc.

With my smile, a positive attitude and positive people around me, I was ready to love my inner self.

During my journey, I realized how I had gotten into situations that were not good for me.

I realized that I needed to love and appreciate my inner self. I had to let go of the hard shell that I had built up around myself in response to all of the things that had happened to me in my life.
The hard shell that I had built was quiet and sad. I had developed it as a child.
I had been an outgoing kid until two heartbreaking things happened to me.
First my mother had a party and while she was briefly in the kitchen, I danced and told some jokes to her friends. As soon as my mother came out I left the room.

Her friends seemed to like it. A few days later I was sitting on the floor while my mother combed my hair. One of my mother's friends from the party called asked to briefly speak to me.

I spoke to her and reprised some of my punchlines from the party for a few seconds. The lady laughed, I said goodbye and gave the phone back to my mother.

I smiled to myself thinking, "Life is good. I love parties and people. I can make it through the boring times and the sad times by looking forward to parties."

Just then I felt my head yanked down. My mother had used one of my fresh tight ponytails to bend my neck over so that she could speak directly into my ear. I was instantly frightened.

She put her lips close to my ear. She spoke in a deep authoritative tone through her clinched teeth.
She said "Listen to me! When people come here, they aren't coming to see you. Nobody wants to see you!"

I can still feel her hot misty breath going into my ear and the strain in my neck. Her words echoed in my mind.
"No one wants to see you… No one wants to see you…" I listened to the echoed.

I took her words as a confirmation that I was weird. I had suspected that I was odd because I seemed to like things that other people weren't interested in. I liked to act out the words of songs and pretend to write letters at my nightstand. I had never seen anyone else doing that.

I had only showed my true personality at the party because the guests had asked me to. When they seemed to like me, I thought maybe that I was special.

When my mother told me that no one wanted to see me I believed my fears that I was just weird. I lost all hope for myself, parties and people.

"Yes Mommy." I said as I sat up soberly. I believed then that the best thing to do around people was nothing. I believed that my natural instincts were wrong.

I began to build my hard outer shell and deny my inner self. My inner self was outgoing but I decided that I needed to be quiet and introverted. The first layer of my outer shell was made of quiet self-loathing.

The second heartbreak that helped me build my outer shell came when my extremely young parents allowed me to walk home from school.

In Kindergarten, there had been a day when no one came to pick me up until hours after school was dismissed. My grandmother had shown up at 4pm when I had been waiting alone on the playground since noon.

My father had apologized for forgetting that it was his responsibility that day. I never held that against him because he was in and out of town so much that he really didn't remember.

By first grade my older sister was assigned to walk me home. Unfortunately for me, my sister liked to socialize with the afterschool program kids and I would have to follow her around for what seemed like hours every time.

The older kids would tease me for being a baby. It wasn't too bad but I began to think that I could walk myself home and avoid annoying the big kids.

It was only four long city blocks from the school to my house. I asked my mother if I could walk home alone.

"Are you sure you can handle that?" She asked me.

I was six years old so I said "Yes Mommy. I will look both ways before I cross the street."

My mother said, "Okay. If you think you can do it, you can walk home by yourself. Be careful."

"Okay Mommy" I said.

I really loved first grade. At the end of class the teacher would roll in a television, turn down the lights and turn on *The Electric Company*. It was an educational TV show that was for kids.
 My favorite part of *The Electric Company* was the Spiderman spoof at the end of the show.
At the end of the show, we would put our chairs on the tables and be dismissed.

In the beginning, I loved heading straight home from school alone, without having to wait for my older sister. Things got better and better until one day when something strange happened.

When I exited the school's gate, two older boys followed me until I crossed the street from school. One seemed to be in middle school and the other in high school.

As I walked, I could hear them referring to me but I didn't understand what they were talking about.

When I looked back at them they just stared and said nothing directly to me. I decided to look forward and ignore them. I was very uncomfortable but when I crossed the street they stopped following me. I looked back and saw them standing on the corner still staring at me. I didn't understand why they were paying attention to me and no one else.

That night I told my mother what had happened in detail. She seemed to think about it for a while. Then she said, "Tomorrow if you see the boys, tell an adult"

I agreed that I would. I felt confident that her advice would prepare me for the next day. I went to school. I watched The Electric Company and the Spiderman spoof. I put my chair on the table and I left the school building and the school gate.

By then I had forgotten everything about the day before and I walked in a group with other kids. I felt safe.

When I neared crossing the street, I noticed the two older boys behind me. They were quiet this day.

I remembered that the day before, they had only followed me until I went across the street. I assumed that they would leave once I crossed the street again. I imagined that I would then go home and tell my mother what had happened when she came home that night.

When I crossed the street, the larger boy grabbed me. The kids who were near us didn't seem to notice. They kept walking. We were on a major intersection in Los Angeles, in front of a church.

The bigger boy pushed me down to the ground and held me there. He told the smaller boy, "Okay, do it to her!"

I was paralyzed with shock. I bucked my eyes and looked up at the smaller boy who was standing monumentally over me.

I watched him kneel down with a worried look on his face.

The older boy had told the younger boy to touch me and violate me. I was six and a half. When it was over, they disappeared.

I was left lying on the ground. I could hear someone singing and shaking a tambourine in the church.

I started to have a conversation with myself. There was a new voice in my head from the outer shell.

I asked, "What happened?"

It said "I don't know"

I asked, "Why did they do that?"

"I don't know but it's your fault they chose you out of all the kids." My outer shell said.

"What do I do now?" I asked.

"Get up" it said.

"How?" I asked.

"Just get up" it said

"What do I do?" I asked.

"Go home." It said.
"Should I go into the church for help?" I asked.

"No, don't bother them, they're happy" it said.

"When I get home should I tell?" I asked.

"Probably not' it's your own fault that you are a bad girl now. You never should have asked to walk yourself home." It Said.

When I got home and for far too many years I told no one about what happened to me.

Physically, I was fine. I still had my virginity and innocence. Emotionally, I was torn. I continued the same type of conversation that I had had immediately after the sexual assault in my head whenever I needed to make a decision or be around people.

The questions were asked and answered in my own head and I lived with constant shame.

I was ashamed of every question that I'd had. I was ashamed that I didn't know what to do. I was ashamed that there was something about me that caused me to be their victim.

I was heartbroken by the sexual assault. The second layer of my hard outer shell was a critical questioner in my mind that always received a shaming answer.

I began to hide my true feelings. I wouldn't allow myself to make decisions with confidence. I began to fear people.

I never told anyone what happened to me until I was an adult and I noticed six year old girl. She was so innocent. She needed protection. I realized that there was no way that I could have caused the boys to choose me. There was no way that I could have known what they would do.

Looking back I think I was the victim of a gang initiation.

I called my mother and I cried and I finally told her what happened to me.

She apologized to me for not noticing that something had happened to me.

Finally, I lost some of the shame that had led me to create my outer shell. I started to remember who I was before I began to live in the shell. I remembered who I was inside before these things had happened to me. I wanted to reclaim my joy and connect with my bliss.

When I began my transition to connecting with my B.L.I.S.S., I had to conquer my own hard outer shell to reconnect with my inner self.

For many years I was a falsely introverted and sad girl. I think I may have been attracted to Destiny's father because he was a good buffer between me and the rest of the world.

I had ignored the red flags from his lifestyle, friends and behavior because I loved having the safety of our relationship.

Once I had Destiny, I knew that I had to do something better for my life. I remembered how much my mother's unhappiness and distractedness had hurt me as a child. There was no way that I could have been happy watching my mother suffer. I knew that a good mother had to be a happy one. I decided to improve myself and my life.

I had to reconnect with my natural instincts and reclaim my joy. I needed to tap into my natural gifts and personality. No one can be successful alone. I needed to be a better person to attract better people into my life.

I took the steps that I needed to take to overcome my situation. I did the work. It was an inside job. Then I developed a method to help other people heal themselves and their lives.
This book contains the information and the techniques that I learned along the way.

My story doesn't define me. I defy my story. I have transformed my life. I dedicated my life to achieving success and leaving the pain behind.

I don't regret one moment of my life. I know that everything that happened led me to be who I am now. I love who I am now so I wouldn't change a thing.

I overcame the pain and reconnected with my B.L.I.S.S. If I did it, you can too.
There are so many benefits to B.L.I.S.S. such as:
- Self-love
- A support team
- Positive, supportive Friends
- Attracting a man who wants to love you
- Freedom from the emotional scars of the past
- Anger management skills
- Money management skills
- Leadership skills
- Guidance to help with parenting
- A fulfilling career
- Confidence

By the grace of God I have found my peace and my bliss. I never want another woman to find herself in the situation that I was in and have to figure it out on her own.

I have broken through to baby momma to find my bliss. I am a successful single mom and now I help other women to find their B.L.I.S.S.

What doesn't kill you does make you stronger. I say baby momma bliss today because I credit my baby momma situation with helping me. If I hadn't had my rock bottom moment with the baby momma label, I wouldn't have gotten my life to the point where I could focus on helping others.

Contents of Baby Momma Bliss

First you will meet Baby Momma Tiffany, a composite client of mine. Her story is a typical one. She was suffering from her baby momma situation. You will take the journey with her through her first steps to single mom success.

I helped Tiffany along her journey with my Breakthrough Life Inspired Success Sessions (B.L.I.S.S.)
The B.L.I.S.S. Sessions inspired the next section of the book which is Baby Momma Bliss (BMB) Wisdom. BMB Wisdom quotes are the keys to ending the suffering of a baby momma situation and entering Baby Momma Bliss.

There are sections focusing on relationships, dating, anger management and money management.

Enjoy this book and please share it with your friends. Share what you learn in life with others. I love you for reading this book and taking your journey with me.

You may contact me through my website: TanyaTalley.com

Blessings of Bliss,
Tanya

Baby Momma Bliss

I made it to Tiffany's beach house around 10am. When I reached the see through glass doors at the top of the stairs I could see her inside using her computer at her desk. She was holding a coffee mug and twirling her hair around her finger.

I knocked and she slowly turned around. Tiffany was gorgeous. She had the perfect height and weight proportions to live in a beach city of Los Angeles. She was wearing a tight white scoop neck sweater and a pair of blue jeans. As she stood up her perfect hourglass figure was revealed. I noticed that her eyes were low and droopy as she walked toward me.

"Hi Tanya, how was the drive over?" she said as she opened the door for me. Her voice was friendly but there was no smile on her face.

We exchanged small talk about my drive over and the morning traffic. Then we sat down together on her oversized white sofa.

"Can I get you a cup of tea Tanya?" she asked.

"Yes, thank you." I said breathing in the tasty smell of her pumpkin spice toasted pecan scented candles that were burning.

I was thinking to myself that no one as nice and beautiful as her should have any problems. I am sure that millions of people would look at this woman and think the same thing. She's living at the beach with a perfect body, plenty of money and plenty of time. She was living the American dream.

All of the women I'd worked with before were living in the inner city. They were dealing with "baby momma trauma." They were lacking what they needed because they were dealing with men who didn't' keep their promises. They were struggling to make ends meet.

Why would Tiffany need my help?

We had only had a couple emails and calls between us to set up this initial consultation meeting. All that I knew was that she was the single mom of a beautiful doll of a daughter. She was referred to me for success coaching by a mutual friend who is a former client.

She knew that I had coached other single mothers to start their own businesses, to endure a legal battle, to find a new romantic partner and more. She needed help with launching a new career and clearing up the mess between her and her child's father.

"Okay, so how have things been?" I said with a smile.

Tiffany took a deep breath and started to tell me her story:

"Tanya, I don't know why I am so angry at my daughter's father and that b*tch that he is with now. I want to get over it, but I can't. I'm working day in and day out and I don't feel like I am getting anywhere. My daughter's father doesn't help me at all. He says that he loves her but all he does is stress me out. Whenever I try to get him to provide the support that we both know that Shayla needs he just says terrible things to me. He causes so much stress in my life. I am the only one who our little girl has to take care of her and he is stressing me out. Stressing me out to the point where I am having headaches, my hair is falling out and I am living on three hours of sleep. Then there's Shayla, she doesn't sleep and she is having tantrums and…"

"Okay hold on just a second." I interrupted. Tiffany's tirade was revealing all of the symptoms of her problem. Tiffany was telling the story of what had happened to her and all of her burdens.

I could understand why Tiffany was tired. I could understand her anger too.

As I listened to her I knew that she had been carrying this story alone for a long time and that it was important for her to tell me what happened to her.

I said to Tiffany. "Why don't you tell me how you got here Tiffany? Of course your situation with your daughter's father started with a relationship. What happened?

Tiffany took another deep breath, started twirling her hair and said, "Tony was an entertainment Lawyer. Do you know what that means? He worked with all of the big names and made the big money. He was an "A list" attorney.

Every woman in the office wanted to ride in his Porsche and ride his pony; the one in his pants. Ha!

There was so much competition for Tony's attention that I never even tried until I realized that he would make a good candidate.

The gossip about him included that he was very family oriented. He even had a picture of his mother on his desk. Tony had no children and was making 8 figures easy. His best friend was the financial advisor who was known for helping the rich become richer and richest. Tony had it all.

I wore my favorite suit to work the day after my 26th birthday and I caught his eye. Yes!

Tony was a tall, handsome charmer. He had the sexy smile that can always get a yes.

He flirted with me and I flirted back.

One day he was standing behind me while I leaned over his desk. Sweet Peach! He said under his breath.

"What was that?" I asked. He did not repeat himself. He knew that I'd heard him.

He liked my sweet peach, my derriere. Whenever I came into his office I made sure that he saw my best asset. I strategically wore my most bootylicious skirts.

He noticed because one day he started calling me peachy. I liked the nickname. It made me feel hot. This was my first nickname since my dad used to call me sweetie pie.

My dad left my mom when I was twelve years old. I stayed with my mother. My father called me during the first year. I didn't want to talk to him. I was a very angry girl and I believed everything that my mother said about him.

He stopped calling for me the second year after he left. My freshman year of high school is when I realized that I missed him more than anything. That was also when I realized that my mother was an alcoholic and a liar.

The rest of my childhood was spent taking care of my mother and trying to keep her out of trouble. She still lives with me today in my guest room. Whenever people see my mother they are shocked because I am corporate and she looks like the drug addict that she is now.

My mother has always lived with me. When I started my flirtation with Tony at work it was the highlight of my existence. Tony chose me. He told me that I could call him anytime about anything. One Valentine's Day I was alone and sad so I called him.

He was alone. He picked me up in his sexy car and took me to his sexy house. After a couple drinks and shrimp skewers we had sex.

I didn't let him take off my panties until he promised that this wasn't a one-time thing. He said "I want you now and I want you to be only for me."

"You want me to be your girlfriend?" I asked.

"Yes! Be my girlfriend, Tiffany." He replied.

"Say it again" I said feeling a rush of passion.

"Be my girlfriend, Tiffany" He whispered into my ear.

He said it again and again. I had the best orgasm of my life from his words.

He gave me validation, the security of a relationship, and mind-blowing great sex –all on Valentine's Day.

I felt so alive with my new boyfriend. He was a man who I could really look up to. He came from a good family too.

I asked Tony about our future together. He would say, "You don't have to worry, I am not going to leave you, ever."

I asked him about marriage and he would say, "Yes, sometime down the road." Or "There is no need for us to get married now."

I spent more and my time at his place. I made or ordered dinner every night. I started to feel like we were married already.

I began to think that a baby would be the perfect reason to make it official.

Family was number one for Tony and he had already begun treating me like I was family. Tony was very protective of his family and he always made sure that he provided what they needed.

One night I asked him, "What would you do if I had your baby?"

"Take care of it and marry you" he replied.

In the morning during sex when Tony was about to pull out I hugged him and whispered, "Let me have it."

He did.

9 weeks later I held the stick that changed my life. Well actually the stick that changed my life was Tony's because I fell in love with it. This stick was my positive pregnancy test.

I was excited happy and scared to death at the same time. Even though I was a grown woman and she lived with me, I wondered how I could tell me mom.

I decided to tell Tony first.

That night I went to his house. He was lying on his back in bed with his hands behind his head. I sat on the edge of the bed. I looked down into his eyes and I told him, "I am pregnant with your baby."

He didn't even sit up. He closed his eyes and said, "I will help you take care of it."

I sat there wondering what he meant for a moment. Then he said "What do you want to do?"

"Keep it" I said.

"Okay then we will keep it." He replied.

I immediately felt a new bond with Tony. "Now are a family" I thought.

Tony didn't want the office to know that I was pregnant so he suggested that I quit working. I did. He paid my bills.

When my mother found out that I was pregnant she asked me why I didn't make him marry me first. She said that if my dad hadn't married her she wouldn't still be getting his social security checks after his death my freshman year of college.

My Mother wasn't happy for me but I was used to that. She was excited about the baby and happy that she was about to become a grandmother. I was glad that my mom would be around to help me during my pregnancy. Other than Tony, she was all that I had.

Tony was more focused on work than ever during my first trimester. He said that he was working on big deals to secure the baby's future.

We didn't see each other as much. I was happy to have a part of him growing inside of me. I loved Tony so much I wanted to have a piece of him with me forever.

I spent more time with Tony's mother. She told me stories about what Tony was like as a baby.

I ordered everything that I wanted for the baby and Tony would pay for it.

During my last trimester I was happy at home with my mother helping me. Tony was out of town on business a lot.

When he was in town he was very distant and distracted. He said that he needed to focus on work and I gave him his space. I started sleeping at my house unless he called me to come over.

One night Tony didn't answer his phone when I called. It got later and later and he never returned my call.

I felt like a silly school girl. I was so worried because he missed one call. I couldn't ignore it. I knew that he was in town. A murky black cloud formed in my stomach and spread into my chest. It was hard for me to breathe when I tried to relax and forget about Tony.

I knew that something was wrong. I felt the same way that I did the day that my father left us. He was supposed to pick me up from school that day. When my mother picked me up she said that everything was okay but I knew that there was something wrong.

I was 38 weeks pregnant. I drove myself 5 miles in the rain to his house. I knocked on the front door. There was no answer. He must be upstairs in the back bedroom. I could feel it in my bones that he was there and something was going on.

I walked around and went through a side gate. I knew that had a tendency to leave a particular side door open. I checked it and it was unlocked. I was dripping wet from the rain when I finally made it inside.

His grey stone, silver metal and shiny glass house would have been freezing if someone hadn't turned on the heat.

I wanted to yell Tony's name and let him know that I was climbing the stairs but another part of me knew that I wanted to see what was keeping him from answering the phone for me. No more excuses.

Was he really working on a case and making plans for our future or was it something else?

When I got to the top of the stairs my adrenaline kicked in. My heart raced, my palms began to sweat and I grabbed the bedroom doorknob and opened the door.

During a split second I saw everything. The room was a mess all of the luxury pillows that I had chosen were strewn all around the room on the floor along with towels. The room was muggy. It was steamy from the shower that was running in the bathroom with the door wide open.

Tony was looking up into the eyes of the golden skinned young woman who was riding him cowgirl style.

I stood there frozen in silence. I saw him having sex with her and enjoying it. I saw love in his eyes. He was focused on pleasing her.

I felt a heavy pressure in my belly and in my chest.

I felt like I could fall apart into pieces. I was shattered.

His cowgirl stopped riding and looked at the black lacquer headboard. She was straining her eyes to see me in the reflection. Then she quickly turned and looked at me

I noticed that she was a Latina receptionist from another office. Her naked breasts were huge and round and perfect.

She screamed and jumped up taking the sheet. Tony was left lying on the bed naked still fully erect. He looked confused until he saw me standing near the door.

"What is wrong with you?" "What are you doing?" "Does she know that you have a baby on the way?" I yelled

Tony looked scared and confused and he sat up.

I picked up everything that I could grab a hold of and threw it at them.

Tony jumped up and wrapped his arms around the girl. He protected her from the hurled objects. He ushered the naked girl into an adjacent room and instructed her to lock herself in and wait while he handles "the problem."

When I heard him refer to me as "the problem" I knew that that was all that my pregnancy had ever been to Tony.

As I stood there I realized that he had never loved me. He could only love this girl who was riding him while he ignored my calls.

I yelled and fought with Tony for hours and his naked Latina never came out of her safe room. He didn't answer any of my questions. He just insisted that I go home and relax because of the baby.

I was hysterical. I couldn't think straight. He walked me to my car and went back into the house with her.
I don't know how I made it home from his house. It was foggy, rainy and my eyes were filled with tears.

I went home that night and I have never been back inside his house again. That receptionist that was on top of him became his new girlfriend.

She is smug and rude to me. I will never forgive that b*tch because she said that she would be my daughter's stepmom and she would raise my child with Tony.

Since she has been in the picture I need to have prior approval and receipts for any purchase that I make if I want money from Tony.

The day that I had the baby there was a huge fight between my mother and his mother and his girlfriend.

Shayla is beautiful and perfect. She's a handful now that she is three but we made a beautiful girl.

Tony threatens me whenever I ask for more money or help. He threatens to take Shayla. I know that he has the type of lawyer friends who could definitely help him take her away.

Most of the money that I get for child support goes to renting our house and childcare.

His b*tch girlfriend doesn't want me to have any support and she makes him fight me on every support increase.

Tanya, now do you see why I love my daughter but I hate him. I hate him and I hate that b*tch.

I'm stressed out. I am tired all of the time. I have migraine headaches. I can't go back and work in his office. I don't want to work in any lawyer's office any more. I don't think that was ever what I wanted.

I haven't had a boyfriend in three years. I have had about three dates. My daughter is a handful she is very active. Sometimes I just wish that I could get a break from everything. I feel numb inside. I know that I am so disconnected that it isn't good for me or Shayla but I'm overwhelmed and overworked.

I know that I am supposed to do everything but I am tired Tanya. I have migraine headaches, my neck is in knots and I am too tired to get out and get another job. It's not fair and I am angry. I am so angry Tanya because when I do send Shayla to see her father he makes sure that I have to see that cheap as secretary that he is with now

He gets a break whenever he wants it. The just went on a Mediterranean Cruise and posted all the pictures on Facebook. She's walking around in her bikini and having fun and I can barely afford to keep my head above water."

In her beautiful home, with her great looks and her precious daughter, Tiffany was living baby Momma drama. A mess! I am sure that she wanted to break Tony's windows out. She and his girlfriend had even had screaming matches in front of Shayla.

All of the baby Momma trauma signs were there:
- Lack of support
- intense Anger/resentment toward Ex/child's father
- Regret
- Financial issues
- poor communication
- tiredness
- Stress headaches
- preoccupation with Ex and Ex's girlfriend
- custody battles
- lack of trust

Baby Momma	Baby Momma Bliss Breakthrough to Single Mom Success
Baby Momma/Wifey	Wife or successful Single Mom
Broke	Wealthy
Recipient	Benefactor
Lonely	Host of friends
Tired	Full of energy
Pouty	Smiling
Voiceless	Advocate
Foolishness	Wisdom

Ignored	Respected
Underemployed	Purpose driven career

Tiffany was living the baby momma stigma. She was barely making it. It wasn't fair.

Worst of all, Tiffany was spending most of her time thinking, wondering and worrying about other people. She was investing nearly no energy into herself at all.

Yes, she needed to deal with her daughter's father but she was obsessed with everything that he did. She was busy trying to figure him out.

This was the plan for Tiffany:
- Improve her relationships: cut codependent relationships, build a support team, healthy dating.
- Improve her emotions/health: Get anger management skills, reclaim her joy, get hobbies, and enjoy life.
- Implement model parenting for a happy child
- Set personal goals
- Find Tiffany a way to get paid to do what she loves
- Find Tiffany's   B.L.I.S.S.

Notice that none of her plan is centered on her ex-boyfriend. Here are the steps that Tiffany went through with me as she became a single mom success and found baby mama bliss:

Breaking through the games

The Baby Momma/daddy situation often contains games. The games are played by the child's mother and father. Once he knows that he is no longer welcome to your bed; he plays the game by beginning a competition. He wants to show you that his life is better without you. Maybe he has a new girlfriend. He will do things to insinuate the idea that he treats this new girl better or that the girl is better than you were.
Mothers can play the game with angry outbursts, busting out car windows and calling his new girlfriend. If she has a new boyfriend she can instigate a fight between her ex and her boyfriend. The baby momma/daddy games only hurt the momma, daddy and baby.
Dealing with a man who promised to help you and is now doing everything that he can to hurt you is enough to spark some serious disgust for that person. It is perfectly reasonable to hate a man who is playing games with your emotions by lying to you and flaunting another woman in your face.
He is doing everything to make you believe that everything that you want and need from him is actually going to this supposedly _____ (fill in the blank: fresher, younger, better cooking, sexier, friendlier, richer, smarter, more beautiful) woman who he is with now.

He IS a jerk for doing this and he is wrong. However you cannot afford to entertain the negative energy by loathing him and his new girlfriend or his mother.

Unifying your House

"A house divided won't stand"

Having a piece of Tiffany's daughter's father in her house all day was driving Tiffany Crazy. It is her daughter Shayla. She looks like him and somehow she sometimes does things the way that he would. Shayla even comes back form visitation smelling like his cologne. Shayla's dirty clothes hamper holds her father's scent like a sachet.

Tiffany did hate him when she had to talk to him about visitation. She hated him when she saw him. She hated his smell on her baby and in her room. She even hated seeing him in the twinkle of her daughter's eyes.

It was perfectly within her right to hate him. He did lie to her, knock her up and cheat. Now he was fighting her to get out of giving her child support while he was clearly supporting his new girlfriend. Do you want Shayla to grow up in a house of love or hate? I asked Tiffany.

"Of course love Tanya but it is his fault." She replied. "When Shayla grows up and tells the story of how her mother was full of hatred, will you be okay with that as long as she mentions that you were also a victim of her father?" I asked sternly.

Tiffany looked off into the distance and daydreamed a minute. When she looked back at me I continued. "You see Tiffany, we all have our stories. You have told me stories about your mother. You told me your mother let life problems break her down. Your mother wasn't emotionally there for you. You were left to fend for yourself when you needed help. Now you have a choice. You may choose to remain the same and keep your anger. Your anger and hatred for her father will definitely come between you and Shayla. Your anger and rage will eventually leave you helpless. Or you can choose to be open to discover something different, a way of looking at things that will set you free from so much of your suffering and will connect you with Shayla in a new way.

The choice is yours. Choose to stay the same and call some friends and complain or say yes to a change and I will help you to the other side of these feelings."

We sat in silence for a moment.

"I am open to something new." Tiffany said with a smile.

With Tiffany's permission, I took her through the steps of unifying her home.

Step one was to separate Shayla from the things that she hated about her father without separating Shayla from her father.

Of course a child is not totally exactly like one parent. Kids take some things from one parent, some others from another parent and then they have their own uniqueness too.

Step one: I had Tiffany write down every good quality or strength or skill that she knew that Shayla's father had. He had many good qualities; high IQ, sense of humor, charming and good grades etc.

Now Shayla isn't forced into being like her father but she has the DNA source or opportunity for these good things.

I instructed Tiffany to make affirmation statements with feeling whenever she would begin to feel resentment toward Tony, in Shayla's presence

When Tiffany would think, "Shayla is screaming and being rude just like her dad. I hate him."

We agreed that she would affirm that "My daughter is a blessing of joy in my life. As I support her, she will overcome challenging behavior."

A few days later Tiffany told me that she was having a great time brushing Shayla's hair when Tony called. During the call her blood boiled.

As soon as she hung up from the call, Shayla started acting up. Shayla bumped a table and knocked down an antique teacup which cracked as it hit the floor.

All of the anger that was inside of Tiffany from the phone call got connected with Shayla. Tiffany wanted to scream. Then she remembered what we had talked about. She took a deep breath to relax. After she helped Shayla calm down and cleaned up the teacup she said some positive affirmations bout Shayla.
"Your father gives you a good source to do very well in your studies. You will be successful in anything that you choose." Tiffany said under her breath to herself.
She told me that she immediately felt better and was able to get back to feeling good much quicker than usual.
Tiffany had taken the negativity of her ex out of her house. This was her first step to bliss.

Over time we worked with the courts to set rules for what Tony could do and say to Tiffany over the phone. This helped Tiffany to avoid a lot of her ex's negativity.
The work of forgiving Tony actually began with the work of Tiffany forgiving herself. Listing Tony's positive qualities helped her to see that she had good reason to trust Tony when she met him. A lot of Tiffany's pain came from her anger at herself. She felt like a fool because she had a child with a man who cheated on her. Listing the many good qualities of Tony helped her to have some compassion for herself.

When Tiffany told me about all of the custody and child support games that Shayla's father played I wasn't surprised. Tony had told the court lies in attempts to get sole custody of Shayla. He would tell Tiffany that he would pay for a class or a medical expense and then later he would have his new girlfriend answer the phone and say that he was too busy to answer.
I wasn't surprised that this man who was so mature in the beginning of the relationship had turned so petty. They say that all is fair in love and war. Many times the baby momma trauma is a custody and child support war.

Some men or women who have certain issues will play a war to win. They don't seem to care who gets hurt in the process. Some men can shut down their feelings and drop atomic bombs on their own child's mother or father. They can say that the mother is unfit or a drug addict when it isn't true. The mother can say that the father is abusive when it isn't true. Do your best to avoid war with your ex and never play emotional games. Keep your child's best interest in mind. The child wants a happy mother and father even if you two are apart.

Tiffany and Tony were both attempting to fault each other's parenting in court. When Tiffany chose happiness she decided to start negotiations over with Tony via mediation. After I talked with her I realized that she actually trusted Tony and his girlfriend with Shayla. She never wanted Shayla to visit when Tony was at work so they had his scheduled entered into the court papers.

Tiffany didn't want Shayla around Tony's girlfriend at all but she compromised because the girlfriend wasn't actually putting Shayla in danger. The court also ordered everyone to communicate only when necessary relevant to Shayla's interest.

After taking these steps, Tiffany had less court drama and Tony agreed to pay more child support.

Baby Momma B.L.I.S.S (BMB) Wisdom

BMB Wisdom: **Cut Co-dependency**

You have what it takes to make it in life, so does everyone else. Let people work out their own issues. Help if you can but don't force it. If you need help realize that you have options. Be creative. Don't get focused on helping or getting help from one person.

Codependent relationships are where you get addicted to someone else's drama. It is also when you put more emphasis on someone else's needs and situations than your own.
Tiffany had codependent relationships with her mother, her daughter's father and a few other people. Tiffany's mother was an alcoholic. Every day her mother would come to Tiffany's house because she needed money. First Tiffany would say "No, I am not going to help you drink anymore."
A few hours would pass and her mother (Brenda) would complain. Tiffany would feel bad and give her mother some money. Then Tiffany would feel bad that her mother left to go and drink. Brenda would come back the next day and start over again until eventually she would get another DUI and end up in jail.
Tiffany felt trapped because she felt bad when she didn't give her mother money. Sometimes her mother would help her and she felt obligated to help her mother.

This was a huge problem so I simply laid out the facts about codependency for Tiffany and I allowed her to decide how to move forward.

Tiffany decided to have an intervention for her mother. I helped Tiffany gather the intervention team which consisted of a professional interventionist, staff from a rehab center and other close family members.

I didn't attend the intervention, but Brenda went away to treatment and came back ninety days clean. Now Tiffany is doing a better job of setting boundaries with her mom and they are getting along better.

Adjusting her relationship with her mom went a long way toward helping Tiffany to fix all of her codependent relationships. She learned that she doesn't have to take care of anyone before herself. Only her daughter is her dependent. She can help people when it will benefit her and them. Giving shouldn't make you feel guilty or trapped.

Parenting without Co-dependency

When I was a kid a made some decisions about the type of parent that I would become when I grew up. I decided that I would never allow my child to feel overlooked the way that I had growing up. I decided that I would focus my entire life on my child.

I think that I was only partially right about my childhood parenting decisions. I still focus on caring for my child so that she knows that she is supported and loved, but I don't put anyone's needs before my own because it just isn't healthy.

Tiffany would get Shayla dressed while she was burnt out and undressed. Tiffany would feed Shayla while was starving. Tiffany took Shayla to play with her friends while feeling terribly lonely.

We must care for our kids in spite of how we feel. However, over time we send a mixed message if we neglect ourselves.

When we forget self-care, we are teaching the kids to be codependent. We teach them to take care of others instead of themselves.

When we do this we are teaching ourselves that feeding our child can take the place of us eating. Taking little Michael or Mary on a play date can take the place of having a friend yourself.

It all starts out innocently enough. Then helping the child achieve their goal can replace you achieving your goals. This codependent parenting can continue throughout life if it is not addressed and stopped.

The child needs a mom who takes care of herself. The mother must place priority on meeting her own needs. "Why?" you ask.

Here is the answer: **As parents our primary job is modeling a happy and successful adult.**

It is important to remember is that our primary job is modeling for our children. So if we do things for the child that we don't do for ourselves, we are teaching our children to be codependent and to do things for other people and not do them for themselves.

Model self-care as a priority and allow the children to perform self-care. It is okay for children to do things for themselves or to wait their turn. Doing things ourselves and waiting are important lessons to learn in life.

In order to make sure that your child's self-care level is appropriate for their age, ask their teacher what a child his or her age should be doing independently at home. Even though my daughter is developmentally delayed due to her autism diagnosis, I keep a child development book handy so that I can reference it to understand the typical strengths of a child her age. It is important to have feedback from a professional such as a teacher or a reference like a child development manual because if you try it is very frustrating to try to teach a child to do something that they are just not ready to do yet. You may think that your four year old is mature enough to brush his teeth with his big brother but maybe his need to feel the texture of the paste or be artistic will override his attention span and he will make a mess.

Working from a child development perspective and teaching the child to do things independently may seem like more work, but once you have begun to focus more on modeling and teaching self-care, the time spent with the child will be much more fulfilling.

Kill Codependency

Let other adults live their own lives and find solutions for their own problems. Set appropriate boundaries between yourself and the other members of your family including the kids. Reconnect with your own needs by asking yourself "What do I need right now" and providing that need and following the steps that are laid out in this book. Remember you have to put the oxygen mask on your face first, breathe and then you can help your child to put his or hers mask on. If you are not breathing, you're not living and you are no help to anyone.

If you find it too hard to fix your codependent relationships, you can get help from your local Codependents Anonymous chapter, find them online at coda.org.

BMB Wisdom: Your children don't want you to sacrifice your happiness for them.

Do you remember what it was like when you were a kid and you could sense that your mother wasn't happy? It's painful. There are many reasons to not give your child the impression that you are suffering for them:

- An unhappy mommy sets up a codependent relationship. They can spend their entire life trying to fix your feelings.
- An unhappy mommy can make the child feel like a burden to you.
- An unhappy mommy is a bad lifestyle example for the child.
- Some sacrifices are necessary and honorable but if you are not happy and enjoying your life, you are doing yourself and child a disservice.

The solution is to do whatever it takes to find the win-win situation of happy mommy and happy child.

BMB Wisdom: Wish him the best.

When I accepted the absence of Destiny's father, I forgave him. I decided to wish him the best.

I believe that we reap what we sow. Put out bad energy and get bad energy.

Unfortunately, Destiny's dad did face an enormous amount of misfortune over the years. I can honestly say that I got no pleasure from it at all. I actually wish him and his family happiness.

BMB Wisdom: Loving You

Once you have disconnected yourself from codependent relationships, what do you do with the energy that you used to use to solve everyone else's problems? The answer is to take care of you and grow in self-love.

A component of the Baby Momma stigma is a lack of self-love. Many of us don't really know what self-love is or what it feels or looks like.

I used to assume that I loved myself because I felt confident at some times, today I know that self-love is so much more than that.

Self-love is the unconditional appreciation of you. Imagine holding a little newborn baby in your arms. You scan their entire being and marvel at it all. Oh look at your little ears and your lips. The baby sighs or turns its head and it is the most adorable thing that you have ever seen. What you are giving the baby in that moment is unconditional love: acceptance and appreciation for who they are completely without expectation or exception. In order to give ourselves love we need to take the same approach

There are some discrepancies among psychologists as to exactly how many we need, but we do need hugs everyday as human beings. I have never seen the number of suggested hugs per day quoted as anything less than 4. Get the exercise, nutrition, rest and hugs that you need every day.
. You also need to pay attention to who you are and appreciate who you find that to be.
Some examples of unique attributes that we can appreciate about ourselves are:
I love to read novels/Reading isn't my thing
I have a button nose/I have a huge honker
I love to feed people/ I don't cook
Notice that the point is not to decide if the thing is good or bad, it is to simply notice and appreciate it. When you appreciate your uniqueness you appreciate your life.
It seems like we have all had that experience where we have looked at an old photo of ourselves when we were younger and thought, "Wow, I was so beautiful, but I didn't feel pretty".
We thought, "I wish that I'd applied myself more in this or that area."
 Well no matter how old we are now, God willing, we will get older and one day and look back at this time. When you look back on now, will you be able to say, "Wow those were some great times and I really appreciated my life?
Whatever we appreciate, appreciates. Whatever we worry about we create.

I am really disappointed when I hear women emphasize what they don't like about themselves. I know that most of us were raised to use self-deprecating humor, but is it worth the laugh to put ourselves down?

Appreciate your life, don't complain about it. No matter what is going on in your life now think about this:

One night I was having a bout of depression, I was so sad. I asked my current fiancé, who I call my happiness mentor, why should I be happy, with so much suffering in the world and with me trying and trying and failing sometimes, why should I be happy? He thought for a second and gave it his best shot and answered with this:

"Of every human being who has ever walked this earth, lived and died, you are alive today." One day you will join the innumerable masses of people who have died. Today and for a limited time, you are alive, be excited and appreciate that, it's amazing. So instead of saying, "My boobs sag lower than before," say "I appreciate that my boobs still look good in this type of bra." Look for and appreciate every little thing about yourself that you like. Not just physically but spiritually, financially, in every way imaginable. Set an example for unconditional love for yourself.

When you learn something that you enjoy doing, add it to you monthly schedule, then weekly and maybe even some element of it daily.

Choose your activities based on what makes your heart soar.

If you think that you are too busy for hobbies, think about the way that you will feel when you are doing the hobby and it should motivate you to make time. If not, then maybe that isn't the best hobby for you. One huge benefit to pursuing your hobbies is spending time with like-minded people. Meeting like-minded people and spending time with them will be a great experience.

If you don't know where to start, think about what your favorite activities as a kid were. Buy some jacks or jump rope. Did you love play dough maybe try ceramics. Break out the roller skates. Write your poems and sing your favorite songs.

Most importantly if you have a message that you want the whole world to know, share it with people. As for me, I never would have known how much I love public speaking, if it hadn't been for Toastmasters International. During my journey to loving myself, I got myself a personal trainer to teach me to take care of my body. During our sessions, she noticed that I loved to give motivational feedback to people and she invited me to a Toastmasters Meeting near my house.

When I first went to the meeting I didn't really understand why I was there but over time I learned that Toastmasters was an organization that had been around since 1924 and was an extremely inexpensive way for a person who loved to motivate people like myself, to get plenty of excellent training in public speaking and leadership.

In Toastmasters I learned to be brave and speak up when I had something to say. I also learned how to be an effective leader and that I love interviewing people. I learned so much about myself there and my self-love increased in the supportive environment.

I also met people who appreciated my uniqueness and mentored me forward.

You see, self-love is about noticing and embracing our own uniqueness unconditionally. Why, because we are all that we have. Again, parenting is about modeling so we must model self-love to our kids so that they can love themselves,

Really our uniqueness is what makes us exciting, it is also valuable. If I had never had my unique experience of feeling like a true Zommy, then I wouldn't have had the material to write this book and let everyone who will ever read it know that if I can go from emptiness to excitement about life then you can too.

BMB Wisdom: Now is when you were so young and sexy and cute

Have you ever found an old photograph of yourself? You think "I was so young and pretty then." "Look at me, I was so cute" "That girl could have done anything that she wanted to."
Truth is, one day you will look at yourself now and think the same thing. Whether you are in your 20s, 30s, 40, 50s or even 60s and beyond, if you still have your health, one day you will look back on now and see that you were young enough to live your dreams. Live your dreams now so that you can be happy when you look back knowing that you did all that you could with your time.

BMB Wisdom: Build up your self-esteem.

This takes time and is an ongoing process but if you give it regular attention it will all work out. Do and say things that make you feel good about yourself. Avoid doing and saying things that make you feel worse. Don't believe the negative things that people have said in the past. Surround yourself with people who really like you and are happy with themselves.

Get out of draining relationships. Follow your dreams. Talk to a good therapist or counsellor if possible. Self-esteem will improve with time.

> **BMB Wisdom:** Get at least 4 to 6 hugs a day.

I remember reading that in the 1980's, during the crack cocaine epidemic, hospitals were taking volunteers to come in and hold the babies that were born exposed to drugs. Without being held, the babies wouldn't develop as well or they would die. We are just grown up babies. Hugs are important, especially if no one is holding you in loving arms all night. If you need to heal your heart from hurts, be sure to get as many hugs as possible.
There is no limit to the power of love. A hug is a chance to give and receive the power at once.

BMB Wisdom: Heal your inner child.

If you experienced a lot of pain or some trauma when you were growing up, you need to heal your inner child. Some people actually communicate with the child which still lives inside of them. You can do this in writing or your imagination. Going to that inner child and giving it the love, protection and support that it needs. I heal my inner child by overcoming the issues from my childhood. You can find techniques in books, online, or you can contact a coach like me to help you.

BMB Wisdom: If you like to get high try to solve the root issue.

If you need to drink or smoke to feel better, find a way to get over the pain. Do inner children work and anger management.

Drinking and drugs only numb the pain for a while. In the long run they actually cause more problems and lower the self-esteem. I have gotten to the point where I stay turned up without chemicals. I am high on the excitement of life. Doing the work works.

BMB Wisdom: Create your support team.

Who can you trust to pick up the kids if you are sick? You better know. Who can you call when you really need a laugh? Go team!

Every mom needs a team, especially if she's single. It takes time to build trust with people and get strong communication with them. When you meet great people, allow them to help you in a way that is natural for them.

You may meet them anywhere. Of course the highest security clearance is required before someone can help you with the kids. However, you can easily add someone to your support team. Just don't get codependent with them and let them do what they do best. In return, they get a great friend like you, or money, return favors etc.

Build a Support Team

To improve your life and breaking through to Baby Momma Bliss, you need to become more resourceful. Resource and relationships go hand and hand. Whether you are in a romantic relationship or not, you need to have relationships with people who are supportive in your life.

Friendly relationships can support you in many ways such as the following:
- Mentoring
- Career advice
- Sales prospects
- Service referrals
- School referrals
- Dates
- Job referrals
- Mentors for your child(ren)
- Much more

Create relationships wherever you go and you will soon have many connections and lots of support.

Meet friends at the following locations:
- Doctor's appointments
- school meetings and drop offs
- extracurricular activities
- the hair/nail salon
- Hobby clubs: crochet, kite flying

- The gym
- Church
- Meditation groups
- Grocery store
- Airport
- Bank

The point is that other people are here to help you. If you are positive and upbeat, you will attract other positive and upbeat people's attention. We attract what we want and what we are into our lives. If you want safe, sane and sweet friends in your life and you are a safe sane and sweet person, you will soon have many friends.

Friends are very important to our status in life. Many studies have shown that our income can be accurately estimated by calculating the average income of the five people who we are with most of the time.

I personally believe that it works for mood as well. If the people that we spend the most time with are complainers, then we most likely are too.

I have surrounded myself with positive and supportive people on a daily basis. I don't have any codependent relationships with my friends that bring me down. I look up to each one of my friends in some way and they all add resources to my life. My relationships are based on mutual respect and admiration. Of course we don't agree on everything and we are not involved in every aspect of each other's lives.

Healthy Friendships

In this world we need friends. As mothers we must have friends. Now that we have forsaken any codependent relationship, friendship should be fun and easy.

One challenge that people face with friendship is that they don't know how to set proper boundaries and feel safe in friendships.

As parents, we must learn to set appropriate boundaries with the people in our lives. We must learn to listen to our heart or our gut about who we allow into our home.

A friend isn't necessary an intimate friend who has access to every part of your life. You may have a friend who you meet at the gym. That person may never meet your family or know where you live. He or she is a person that you share your gym experience with and that's it.

Of course you should have intimate friends who know you very well, but that is not for everyone in your life.

Learn to take what is relational to you about people and allow the rest to be free. I don't attempt to make my friends have the same beliefs as me. I relate to my friends at the places where we connect.

Allowing people to be themselves and be your friend is a good practice for parents. You may have a child who doesn't agree with you, but you can still respect each other and enjoy each other's company.

An easy way to make friends is to strike up conversations with people wherever you are. If you feel a positive connection, then give the person your business card and have them make a note on the back of it, or pull out your smart phones and friend each other via social networks such as Facebook or Linked In.

Remember to keep interactions positive, upbeat, and based on shared interests. Over time a friendship develops and each friendship brings more resources and support.

Appropriate friendships make life sweeter. I remember learning that people who have healthy friendships are less likely to be depressed, when I majored in Psychology in college.

You should be cautious of you allow into your house or around your child, but friends are a support system and every mother should have a strong support system whether she is married or single.

Successful Mom Mindset: Surround yourself with the best! For your success always keep the best people on their team. Your team of friends will influence the opportunities that are available to you and your children.

Get help: sometimes if you don't have any positive friends who support your new habits. You may not be close enough to your new friends to have deep conversations yet. In these situations you may want to turn to a counselor or therapist and open up to him or her.

BMB Wisdom: Become a stronger Leader

Spend some of your time developing your leadership skills. We are all leaders.

We see things that can be improved in situations. We have ideas that others don't have. Instead of doing it all alone or just feeling overwhelmed, develop leadership skills and create a team to get things done. Tiffany wasn't happy with some of Shayla's services. We worked together so that Tiffany could see that Shayla's teachers, doctor and father's family were part of her support team. Tiffany was a leader on that team.

We took on one of Tiffany's goals for Shayla and took steps to lead Shayla's team to the goal:

- Creating a vision for the team.
  "I want Shayla to eat healthier food this semester at school."

- Presenting the vision to the team
  (To team members) "Won't it be great when Shayla is healthy and strong from eating quality food."

- Delegation

    - To the Doctor "Can you suggest a healthy diet for my child?"

    - To the kindergarten Teacher "I am changing Shayla's diet, please let me know if you notice any change in her energy or attention level."
    To the father's family "While Shayla is with you would you please offer her these healthy snacks that I have sent?" "What healthy snacks does Shayla eat with you?"

    - To her friend "Want to come over and help me prepare healthy snacks for Shayla? We can taste them as we go."

    Also
- Follow up and support

- Analysis of progress

- Reward your team (including yourself)

Leadership skills are extremely important because we need to use them every day.

You probably are the person with the most invested in your child's life but you don't have to take care of him or her alone. Carry the vision and set the standard. Foster relationships and create a team to get everything done.

Leadership skills are developed over a lifetime. The Step is to make an effort to improve the skills on a regular basis.

You can improve your leadership skills and expand your networking circles by joining a club in your community. Most cities have women's clubs or nonprofit organizations that welcome mothers. In these clubs you just may find a mentor, friend, fun, and a leadership opportunity.

I personally recommend Toastmasters International to develop leadership skills. The organization's tagline is *"Where Leaders are Made!"*

Toastmasters clubs help you to practice your public speaking and leadership skills. For more information go to toastmasters.org or contact me because I am always happy to share about Toastmasters.

Notice that you are a leader and that you need to hone those skills on a regular basis.

BMB Wisdom: The people at the school are part of your team.

My daughter is in special education. I have experienced of many negative situations in the school system. I have heard many horror stories. I also know that I need to work with the people who are helping teach my kid. I always keep a positive and active role in my daughter's school. Make sure that they know you and they have a good outlook on you.
When it comes to negotiation or issues with the school, bearing cupcakes will get you much farther than cussing people out.
Besides, don't leave your child with someone who is angry with you. My parents did that and I would hear an earful of negativity about them by the time they picked me up.

BMB Wisdom: When the blessing comes back, receive it.

I have noticed that it is harder for me to receive than it is to give. I have a hard time asking for help and I am challenged at times when someone offers to help me. Overcoming these issues has helped me immensely. I let people help me now. Remember the support team. I thank God for my help every day!

BMB Wisdom: Appreciate your team members

Your team is the people around you doing what they can. Appreciate what they can do. Each tiny thing that they do is huge for you. Give them love and acceptance in return.

BMB Wisdom: Build long-term friendships.

Just keep in touch with them from time to time and you will have another person to laugh with about the good old times.

BMB Wisdom: Have a real "No!"

If the answer is no, say NO. You can say no and still be nice. Honesty is the best policy. If the answer is no just say no.

BMB Wisdom: You can always make new friends.

Believe me you can make new friends. There was a time when everyone in my life knew the depressed low self-esteem Tanya. As I changed or even before I changed I began to have less and less in common with some of those friends. I live in Los Angeles County with over 10 million people so maybe it is easier here, but I promise you, you can make new friends if you lose some.

Dating Success

Single Mothers have questions about dating…
How am I supposed to date when I have children at home? When do I introduce my kids to the man that I am dating?
Principles for blissful dating:
Think of dating is like an interviewing process. We share our objectives with each other and see how they match up.
If a guy asks you out for a date, he is offering you an experience. When I was dating I came across a lot of guys who wanted to come over my house.
Unless he is going to do some home improvements or take over my kitchen, I can only think of a few experiences that he is offering me at my house.
Sex is not necessarily part of dating, especially at first. You do not interview someone by having sex with them.
Sex is a contract. That is why it is referred to as sealing the deal.
You have the dates (interviews) and see if you want to accept the terms of the contract. There are so many types of relationships these days. If you have sex with someone, you are immediately in one.

Negotiate the terms of the relationship before you seal the deal based on the type of relationship that you want. You may want one of the following popular types of relationships:
- Marriage: legal documentation of rights to each other till death or divorce.
- Long Term Relationship: Exclusive, serious and endless
- Friends with benefits: Casual, lasting, sexual
- Booty Call: Casual, sporadic, sexual
- No Strings attached (NSA): Anonymous Sex with a chance to become a series of NSA meetings or booty call relationship.

The problem is when we assume what the other person wants. Another problem happens when a woman thinks that sex will make a man want the same type of relationship that she does. You may want a marriage or a long term relationship or even a sugar daddy, and end up with no strings attached. Date before you seal the deal.

During dating and conversation overtime we reveal what we want. Like any negotiation process some skills are needed to get the best deal.
- **Patience**

If you let the other person know what you want most up front, they may use it as a pawn to trick you into giving them what they want. This is why dating can feel like a game.

It is okay for dating to be like a game as long as you don't make the stakes higher than necessary.
Take things slow. Whether you are starting a casual friendship or looking for a husband it all starts with small talk. Reveal yourself slowly as you get to know the **person. When you take it slow you win. There are plenty of interesting conversations to be had before you get into your most intimate facts.**

- **Discretion**

Since dating is like a negotiation, an interview process and even a game, it should not be brought into rest of your life until a relationship is established and stabilized
 Try not to seal the deal until you agree with the terms.

Keep dates safe. Lessen stranger danger. Meet your date in public places during the day if possible until you feel comfortable.
The people we date are just like any other friend until they gain another title. Be careful with the boundaries. Don't immediately bring people into your whole life. Never force your children into a dating situation.

Some single mom's talk to their kids about dating and relationships in hopes that their teenagers will return the favor. In my opinion a mother should leave the dating talk for her adult friends. I don't think that our children should give us relationship advice.

Use your support team to make sure that the children are well taken care of and then go on the date and have fun

Positivity
After looks, I find that I base my perception of people on the "vibe" or vibration that I feel around them. Your vibes are picked up before you say a word. It reflects your attitude.
In life, we get what we give. Give out positivity and receive it back on dates. If you want to have better partners in the future you will need to make a positive first impression and be open to living a positive lifestyle. Leave bitterness behind and out of your dates.

Honesty
If you don't ever tell a potential partner who you really are, what you really like or what really want, they won't ever know.
Faith

Falling in love again can feel scary. In order to overcome the fear and give yourself a chance at love have faith that with the proper boundaries you can handle whatever comes your way.

When you go on a date it should be a fun time. Let this guy show you what it is like to spend time with him. It is a preview of would be like with him. A date doesn't mean that he is your boyfriend now. Things take time. Please have patience my friend. Give dating some time. If you date him for a while things my run their course and end. Or it could last and he may become a member of your team as boyfriend. Take your time and save something special for when he does become your boyfriend.

BMB Wisdom: A DATE IS NOT SOME GUY COMING TO YOUR HOUSE.

Playing house is not a date. A date should be adding something fun to your life. Date safely: Try not having sex while you are dating. If you do need to have sex, then choose someone you can trust and who will treat you well. (I don't know why this guy who you trust and will treat you well isn't your boyfriend btw.)

Meet guys who you don't really know only in public places. Keep your kids out of it until the right time.

BMB Wisdom: Know your Standards

There is someone for everybody. Love yourself enough to wait for a guy who cared about you and meets your standards. In the meantime, dating is fun if you are doing it in a safe way.
You get what you pay for. For instance, dating a married man is never a good thing to do. He needs to get that divorce before you sleep with him. Don't forget that you reap what you sow. karma is real. Criminal guys are getting laid too. Thugs are sexy but they are victimizing people. Do you want to be spiritually connected sexually with a guy who hurts people? Choose a guy who can find a legal hustle.

BMB Wisdom: **Don't lay down with losers.**
Criminals: I have a certain family member who loves thugs. I fixed her up with a couple nice successful handsome guys. Then she admitted to me "Tanya he's nice but I like a thug."

The next thug she dated and had a child with ended up breaking her ribs. After she broke up with him she ended up marrying a prisoner in jail.

If you lay down with dogs don't you wake up with fleas? Lay down with a criminal and you are supporting a predator. He has victims out there and he will reap what he sows. You don't want to have to suffer because of what he has done.

Other types of losers to avoid:

Habitual liars and excuse makers

Multiple family makers (possibly)

Disrespectful

Racist

Etc. and the list goes on;

BMB Wisdom: **Let go of useless relationships.**
Don't force a relationship to exist. If you have nothing in common let it go. If you don't like the person, wish them the best and say goodbye. Maybe you will meet again under better circumstances.

BMB Wisdom: Fall in love again.

It is worth it.
I was afraid to fall in love again after a failed relationship. I was terrified. I thought the new guy was setting me up. Turns out I was falling in love. I am glad that I gave it another shot.

BMB Wisdom: You can't make a man do what he doesn't want to do…

…BUT YOU CAN MAKE HIM WANT TO DO IT.

From my experience, it is a lot easier to help a man adopt the same ideal that you have than it is to force the idea on him.

A man who doesn't want to do something may do it anyway but retaliate later or do a bad job of it.

Don't try to force him to do it. Motivate him to do it. Make it fun. Maybe make it playful.

"Ready, set, go! How fast can you take out this trash?" Is more effective than asking, "Why can't you ever take out the trash?" if you want cooperation.

I have learned this well from my relationships with men. I have shared this gem with some of my friends who have sons and they have said that it applies to their boys too.

BMB Wisdom: Men don't count time with their kids as time with them.

This can cause a lot of confusion. This is a difference in thinking between men and women that causes many issues and breakups.

I was shocked when I confirmed this fact with real men. It is not that they don't appreciate the time; they just aren't getting all their needs met by what you are doing for the kids. They still need attention too.

BMB Wisdom: If your relationship is violent or destructive leave right now.

When I left my daughter's father I was pregnant. I knew that I would keep my baby. I knew that I needed to keep her safe. Hopefully you don't deal with domestic violence or verbal/emotional abuse, but if you do, get help if you need it and get out.

BMB Wisdom Parenting Commandments

This section is a list of best practices for single parenting.

1. Have the kid for the right reason.

Since I am in a happy relationship space now, a few people have asked me will we have a child. My thinking on having a child is as follows:
There are too many people here who don't have parents' loving support.
I shouldn't have a kid to fulfill my need to have a kid with my partner.
I should have a kid because I want to dedicate the rest of my life to providing loving support to another person.
I should not have a baby with expectations of who that baby will be.
I should let the child show me who they are over time as I lovingly support him or her.
Now taking all of those points into consideration, I am not expecting to have another child anytime soon. Your reasons and expectations for having a child may be different but please think of things from the baby's perspective. Just because you want to stay with the father forever and you can afford a crib, stroller etc. doesn't mean that you need to have a baby.

The baby will need love, attention and time from you. The baby will need peace and peace of mind. The baby will need you to be happy and sane.

2. You can't over baby a baby.

Hold the Baby. Baby the baby. Let the baby know you are there. I babied my baby now she is very independent and confident in herself. A baby doesn't need discipline. Give it love and acceptance.

3. You are not your child's mother and father.

You don't have to try to be something that you are not. I know a lady who I will call "Nicole" Nicole always says that she is her children's mother and father. She has even taught her children to give her Father's Day cards and gifts. I believe that her heart is in the right place but her actions are causing some negative side effects.

First of all, the kids actually have a father. Nicole has always complained that the children's father doesn't participate enough. There is a chance that Nicole has done a good job at making the children feel that she is their father and mother. Perhaps the father and the children don't bond because they feel that momma is the real dad.

Also if a father is a man, how can a woman be a father? Why put so much pressure on yourself to be man and woman, masculine and feminine? You already have enough things to handle.

If you are tough with fake masculinity, where will your child get the influence of a female parent?

I remember Nicole telling me how she taught her son to box because he was getting bullied and there was no man to teach him to fight. A male or female boxing coach could teach him how to box, but a man could understand what it feels like to be a boy and get bullied. Years later Nicole's son was arrested to physically assaulting his child's mother. I wonder if he felt that it was okay to fight a woman because he had learned that men and women are interchangeable.

Sometimes single moms want their sons to be tough because they see that as being a manly. I have coached men who were raised to be "tough" by a single mother. Their mothers have physically beaten them. There were never allowed to cry. These men who I have worked with have serious issues with women.

Remember that a son needs a mother too. If you become the father you take the mother away from the child.

Nicole wanted to be everything that her son needed but as we know, "It takes a village to raise a child"- African Proverb.

If you face the fact that the children currently don't have a father it leaves the door open for a step-father, mentor, uncle etc. to come in and help momma and the children.

If there is no father around, connect with some positive role models. Get advice from other successful single mothers when situations arise.

4. Surround yourself with the type of friends that you would want your kid to have as a teenager.

Hopefully your friends encourage you to do healthy things. Hopefully they are trustworthy, respectable and treat you with love.

5. Be the very best mother that you can be and your kids will be ahead of the game.

It has been proven that if a child has a tough family situation they can still be successful and stay on the right path if they have a strong positive relationship with at least one adult.***

We see successful people who didn't grow up in the best situation every day. They usually had one solid adult in their life. That one person in your child's life can be you.

6. Teaching respect is number one.

If you don't stress mutual respect, you're teaching that disrespect is okay. It will be very hard to stop disrespect later.

The worst of it is that kids who don't learn respect grow up to feel empty. They don't appreciate or respect anything. They become sad people.

I don't think that hitting is respectful to kids. I believe spare the rod; spoil the child means to use discipline but not literally beating your child.

Imagine the rod as a band leader's baton and you are leading the way for the kid. If beating a kid worked you wouldn't have to beat the kid over and over. If making your kid afraid of you worked then no child who feared their parent would be in trouble.

Respect isn't fear. If you fear someone, you dread them to come around. When they only obey out of fear, they will rebel when they are alone.

When you use violence you teach violence. Hitting is an immediate solution but it creates a long term problem.

There are many books and tips on the internet about nonviolent parenting and teaching respect.

7. The voice that you use to correct your child will be a voice in his or her head.

Yes. And that critical voice in your head is from someone who criticized you. We think that we are being extra hard on our kid so that he or she can have it better later. The truth is: if you are overly critical with them now then they will be hard on themselves later.

Be honest. But when they make a mistake, emphasize that it's not about the problem, it's about the solution.

I remember as a child, if I did something as easily fixed as spilling water by accident, my parents would scold me for it. I would end up literally crying over spilled milk.

How about some compassion? I let my daughter know that I love her no matter what is going on. I tell her I don't like what she did and she could have made a better decision, but I don't try to make her feel like she is not a good person.

8. Build your child's team with him or her.

Just like you, your child needs his or her own team. You don't need to be everything for your child. Being a great mother is enough work for you. The child needs good friends, mentors, networking connections, hairstylist, references etc. Help them build their team.

Miracles happen every day. (If you or your child needs one)

I remember the day that my daughter was diagnosed with autism. My daughter didn't speak and the doctors said that it was likely that she never would. I prayed and hoped without really seeing any progress for many years.

I never stopped talking to my daughter all day every day even though she didn't seem to be able to speak. Over the years I decided to share the best possible life with her whether she ever said a word or not.

My eyes are tearing up right now as I write this because I am so thankful for the miracle of her voice. . Just last night, my daughter told me, "I want water please." She is beginning to use sentences. Every day she is getting better. I thank God for my miracle.

If you need a miracle, I believe that it will happen for you too.

9. Celebrate your child. Children are a blessing.

Remember how happy you were when you first saw your baby's eyes. They said it was healthy and you had so much joy. Remember how exciting it was to find out that you were pregnant. Let your kid feel that when they come home from school. Give them some special celebration every day, just because they are here.

10. Remember Dumbo's mother.

I am protective of my daughter especially because of her special needs. When I am tempted to go overboard protecting her I always think of Dumbo's Mother. Dumbo from the Disney tale had the huge ears. Everyone else at the circus was making fun of Dumbo. Dumbo's mother went crazy and got locked up as a result.

Once you go off the chain, no one cares why. Think twice before your anger gets out of control. Sometimes people will treat you unjustly and deny your child of what is right. You still need to think because if you are locked up then no one will be there to protect your child from the system.

11. See great things for your kid.

If you can see it they can feel it. If they have a hope or dream, encourage them. You don't have to prepare them for disappointment. Just be there to hold their hand through the process. Disappointments turn into new opportunities if you don't give up. Remember my daughter is diagnosed with severe autism. I see a great future for my daughter and it is happening day by day.

12.   Let your child help you.

Relationships are built through help. Some parents are better at letting the kids help than others are. I don't mean use the child as a slave. I mean if the kid enjoys doing something and they are good at it, let them help. It helps a child have a healthy self-esteem and relationship with you.

Children are helpful.

Remember that the good book says children are a blessing. They are helpful. My daughter has given me valuable insight. I have also made great friends through her. The unconditional love that we share is healing to my heart.

BMB Wisdom: Don't ever bust out his windows.

There is something about baby daddy drama that makes a woman want to bust out her ex's car windows. My friend "Natasha" found out that her children's father had slept with a girl who lived around the corner from her. She went down to his car and kicked out his car windows. In the process she cut her leg very badly and needed stiches. He fixed his windows and she has a nasty scar for life.
He had every right to call the police on her. She would have likely gone to jail. It seems as though it would be so satisfying to hurt something that he truly loves "his car." In reality, once the windows are broken, he will probably take more money away from the child and get his windows fixed. The difference will be that now he has a legitimate reason to call you a basic bitch. Even your neighbors and family may start to think that maybe he is the level headed one of the relationship. Besides, is that the way that you would want your child to address a problem?

BMB Wisdom: Everyone gets angry

It's okay to get angry. When I lead anger management workshops, some people always say, "I don't get angry." When they say that they mean, "I don't yell and scream when I get angry." Anger can be quiet too. I live in Los Angeles where nearly each person has a car and drives. The traffic is challenging. When people cut me off and slam on the breaks I get to practice my anger management skills. I Take a deep breath and realize how I feel. I feel my eyes burning and a tightening in my stomach. I take another deep breath and put things into perspective. He doesn't know me. Thank God I didn't hit his car. One more breath, best wishes to him. I thing "Maybe I will meet him again on better terms."
Being angry doesn't mean that a person is yelling or out of control. It means that something happened and you are definitely having a reaction. Anger is nothing to hide. Anger is something to manage. If you are having trouble with feeling anger there are many self-help   anger management books that can help. If there is a situation or person that causes nearly uncontrollable anger on a regular basis, you may want to get away from that person or situation. Start working on your exit plan if necessary.

BMB Wisdom: Manage your anger.

Anger visits everyone. Anger doesn't always look like screaming and yelling. It can look like you shutting down and being quiet. Anger can be held inside. The key is to notice when you are angry. Don't run from anger. Realize that anger is there as a signal. You can use anger to help you make a different decision in the future.

Anger offers a short term or long term solution. Yelling or fighting can release the anger in the short term; however it ruins everything in the long run. When you are angry try to make decisions that are good for the long run.

For detailed anger management instruction see my worksheet online at **www.tanyatalley.com**

Anger Management

Ever find parking spot, prepare to turn in and someone else swoops into it? A situation like this can cause instant anger.

We all feel anger from time to time. You may say that you don't get angry because they don't yell or get violent with rage. You may be the person who shuts down in anger. A quiet riot is when the anger shows as a withdrawal from conversation and contact. Sadness and depression have been described as "anger turned inward." Anger visits us all.

Single Mothers have lots of good reasons to be angry. It took two people to make the child but we are often left to handle the job alone.

Once you get angry you are side tracked and vulnerable to negativity. In order to reach your goal you must develop good anger management skills. Anger management is not something that we are born with. Anger management is something that is learned. The problem with learning anger management when we grow up is that when we see that people are angry they are typically acting out in a negative way and we learn those negative behaviors. When the people around us are using excellent anger management skills we probably don't notice that they are angry and don't learn to adopt the techniques that they are using.

As single mothers we need to stay on track and manage our anger to overcome the following side effects of anger:
- Health problems (High blood pressure, stroke, heart attack etc.)
- Road rage
- Drug abuse (as an escape from anger or to express anger)
- Depression (anger turned inward)
- Isolation
- Domestic violence
- Poor parenting
- Incarceration

Any of the situations listed above would devastate your life.

F.A.C.T.S.

In order to avoid busting out windows and all the side effects of unchecked anger I have researched and developed *F.A.C.T.S.* steps to anger management which are as follows:

F Identify the **FEELING** that triggered anger (there are a few basic reasons that we get angry)

A **ASK** yourself is that feeling based on facts or fiction

C **CONNECT** with reality

T TALK yourself through it

S Build your **SELF ESTEEM**

When you know that you are angry separate your feelings of anger hurt and rejection from the FACTS and you will successfully manage your anger and improve your life.

F =Identify your FEELINGS

When you feel anger it is real. You will feel:
- A burning sensation inside
- Tightening in your chest
- Tension in your clenched jaw
- Emotionally detached

You may want to yell and throw things. You may want to run away. You may just shut down and try to avoid the situation all together by ignoring it.
You are really angry, but why?
The reasons that you will get angry fall into the following three categories:
1. You feel that something is belittling your self-worth.
2. You feel that something is coming between you and something that you need.
3. You feel that something goes against what you believe in.

When you realize that you are angry the first step to management is to identify what you are feeling. Do you feel like you need to preserve you self-worth, your needs or what you believe in?

You made it to the store. You spot the perfect parking space. You get excited and prepare to turn into the parking space. All of a sudden a brand new sports car swoops in from nowhere and takes the spot that you were so happy to find.

Now you are sitting in your car clutching your steering wheel and you know that you are ANGRY!

We get angry because we feel that something is belittling our self-worth

Are you angry because you feel like the other driver's actions were demeaning to you? Do you think that what the other driver did implied that you were not important enough to respect your presence? Do you feel like the other driver treated you like you didn't even exist?

If the answer is yes, then you have identified the cause of your anger as a perceived belittling of your self-worth.

We get angry because we feel that something is blocking us from getting an essential need met.

As you sit in your car and feel the burn of anger do you imagine that the other driver took your space and you really needed that spot? Do you sit there feeling that the other driver robbed you?
If you answered yes, then you have identified the feeling behind your anger trigger as a need that you have going unmet.

We get angry because we want to preserve our basic convictions.

Are you sitting in your car wondering angrily about how that other driver would be inconsiderate of your needs? Are you thinking "how dare this person do this to someone else?"
If you are thinking like this you are angry because what the driver did conflicts with your basic convictions. What just happened goes against everything that you believe in.
Now that you know what feeling triggered your anger it's time to take the next step

A=ASK yourself are these feelings based on facts or fiction

Now you know that your anger was triggered by your feeling belittled, feeling like you have unmet needs or feeling like something is going against your fundamental beliefs.
The next step is to ask yourself are your feelings based on fact or fiction. Facts are things that are true, fiction is a made up story.

> **Did this belittle me? When I look at the facts was it belittling or is that the story that I am telling myself?**

In actuality the other driver doesn't know me, doesn't have any idea about my self- worth so why would he want to belittle me? The belittling is not fact, it is fiction.

Has this situation caused me to have unmet essential needs? Did the driver actually prevent me from having something that I desperately needed?

The truth of the matter is although you needed a parking space, that particular space wasn't a necessity. Plus the driver probably didn't know that you have a child who is hungry in the car and you only have 15 minutes to run into the store and get out.

The driver took a space that was an option for you not something that you desperately needed. If you drive a little further you may find a better space.

The facts do not dictate that a major need is unmet. Your anger is partially triggered by the story that you have told yourself about what happened.

Does this situation threaten what you believe in?

The driver did something that seems to be very inconsiderate and rude. Most people are offended by rude behavior. If you accept the other driver's behavior it would probably go against everything that you believe in.

The fact is that the behavior was not right if it was intentional. .If what the driver did was unintentional he or she did nothing offensive at all.

This brings us to the next step.

C= CONNECT with reality and CHOOSE a response.

Now that you have asked yourself some questions you should have a clearer picture of the situation.
- The driver does not know you so his or her actions were not related to your self-worth. You have no reason to feel belittled.
- Although you wanted the spot, it wasn't necessarily a need because there are other spots that you can find. The other driver did not take something essential from you. He or she only took an option away.
- If the driver's actions were intentional they went against everything that you believe in, however you don't know if the actions were intentional or not.

Looking at the facts in this way, you can connect with what really happened and choose your response. Now that you have taken a moment to think about things the only issue that is left out standing is whether the driver did this intentionally or not.
You have four choices:
1. Assume that the driver did this intentionally and remain angry as you drive away.
2. Assume that the driver did this intentionally and let him or her know that you are angry by yelling something, honking or driving erratically.

3. Ask the driver if he or she saw you attempting to park and base your feelings on his or her response.
4. Assume that the act was unintentional and seek another parking space.

The fourth choice makes the most sense to me because the person probably didn't see you. With choice four you are safe, you can move on and you aren't left with any negative emotions.

You are not suppressing your anger because you will take step Four.

T= TALK yourself through it

In order to process your feelings it is important to talk your way through acting on your choice. You have chosen to drive away. How do you leave the negative feelings behind?

Originally, we told ourselves a story about what happened and it made us mad. We told ourselves, "This person saw me about to park and then then they came and took the spot that I needed! How could they be so rude?"

Now that you have identified your feelings, asked yourself some questions, Connected with reality and made a choice, it's time to tell yourself a story that will leave you feeling better about the situation.

Now you can say, "That person probably didn't see me. I can find another space. Just like there was a spot for them, there is a spot for me." to yourself.

Your-self talk will be much more effective when you take step five.

S= SELF-ESTEEM

Self-esteem is so important to anger management. The more insecure that you feel about your self-worth, the more you will be triggered to anger. Always take steps to improve your self-esteem and keep it high such as:
- Get enough exercise
- Eat a proper diet
- Excellent hygiene
- Personal development: read books and learn techniques to improve your life.
- Get counseling to help you overcome your issues from your past.

Anger Worksheet

TO HELP TIFFANY I USED THE ANGER MANAGEMENT BLISS WORKSHEET AVAILABLE AT TANYATALLEY.COM. YOU CAN GO TO THE WEBSITE AND USE THE SAME WORKSHEET FOR FREE.

BMB Wisdom: The key to getting through negative emotions is to feel them.

The key is to know that feelings like fear sadness, loneliness and anger okay and normal. You have the right to get angry or afraid.
If you run from the feeling it will get worse. It is like hiding from something vs confronting it. When you are hiding you suffer the entire time. You say "I can't believe this, this is too terrible" to yourself.
Once you allow and acknowledge the feeling it starts to get better. Admit it to yourself. "I feel afraid." That statement will help you get clarity. Your feelings are a message to you. Honor the message of your feelings by acknowledging them and they will decrease. Then feel how the feeling feels in your body. Are you holding your breath? Breathe deeply. Then make some decisions about what to do.
If you feel bad more than you feel good for a few days reach out and get help. Tell a therapist or doctor how you feel.

Anger is okay.

Anger is a good emotion because it lets us know that we need to do something. We need to say something, change something or see something in a different light.
If we saw something threatening our child for instance, we would get so angry that we could us the drive to protect our loved one.
The problem comes when we do something that makes us feel better immediately but makes us feel bad in the long run. The steps listed above to stick to the facts and manage anger in a healthy way.
I still get angry but I don't stay there for long
Things happen on a daily basis to cause our energy to change. We are going about our merry way. We are handling our tasks successfully until we are backing into a parking spot at trader Joes and some inconsiderate b*s**rd backs into the spot that we were obviously going for. Now the happy turned to angry in a flash. The most Zen master in the world is still going to get angry at some point. At this point in my life I still have to deal with anger.

Anger can be described as energy as well as an emotion. It is one face of adrenaline. Anger says fight and Fear says flight. Therefore it is natural, good and conducive to many things. I would attribute anger to the burst of adrenaline or energy that enables a mother to pick a car up to free their child
So what am I supposed to do with that adrenaline and energy to fight sitting inside my car at trader Joes? Get involved with road rage and possible end up on the news as the latest person to be arrested? What I have learned is to change my energy to something that is useful to me. I trigger this change. First I notice my current energy and ask is it useful? Do I need to fight? If you have time to ask that, then the answer is no. So I realize that I am angry because of what happened, but I always remember that just because a feeling was triggered, I don't have to stay in it. I think about my intention for the moment, to get food for my family to have pleasant interactions with other people and to spread positive energy in the universe. I realize that other people's actions may annoy me but they are doing what is real and true for them.

A huge part of the "Baby Momma stigma" is lots of anger. There are many opportunities to get angry during the day of a single mother. The Step is to get out of anger once you get triggered. Some people get cut off in traffic during their morning commute and get mad and carry that anger with them the rest of the day. Some mothers are resentful toward their child's father and they carry it toward their own child, all men or even the whole world.

Learn to recognize and alter your own emotions. For me the remedy to my anger or sadness is thinking of my favorite things.

Today I realize that people act upon their beliefs of what is right at that moment. I don't get angry as often when I realize that people's actions aren't part of a sinister plot to ruin my day.

Managing Money

The cure for the baby Momma stigma is abundance. Get out of the lack and into abundance with the following life changing instructions for your finances, relationships and health. These are the tips that I used to change my life. I learned these things from the people that I chose to use as mentors in my life. I also read books and studied what other people did to change their lives. The best thing about life is that if something works for someone, it can work for anyone. There are many of people who are enjoying success right now. We can do what they have done and create our own success for ourselves.

I started out on my own doing whatever felt good for me financially. I did what felt good to me. Spending felt good to me. I would spend my money when I had it and then try to save it when it got low.
The problem with the "spend then save method" was that I would go into "save mode" when I still had bills due. The only connection between the spending time and the saving time was the worrying. I worried so much about money. I worried about if it would really come. I worried about when it would come. I worried about if I was keeping it safe. I worried about losing it. I worried about if it was enough or not. I worried while I spent it. I worried if I'd spent too much. I would worry all the same things as I held on to whatever were left of the money until I would get some more money and then start the process all over.
In order to get my finances in order I had to kick it old school. When I got tired of the "money go round" I knew that I needed guidance. I didn't really have any friends who I felt comfortable discussing my money matters with so I turned to two other sources. One source was my church. I was a regular member and tither at my local church so I took advantage of the financial training course that they provided. During the course I learned a lot of fundamental financial planning and strategies. I learned about investment income, passive income and residual income.

The course that I took at church offered me many reasons to get on the right financial track. I realized that:
- Money doesn't discriminate. If you make it, it will work for you just like it does for someone else.
- I need to manage my money and not let it manage me.
- I need to pay my bills and savings up front.

Those points helped me a lot. I still needed a system to handle my money. The system that I chose is simple and easy.

The envelope system in steps:
1. Create a budget: Write down all your monthly expenses (food, gas bills, hair stylist, clothes etc.) Then write down all of your monthly income. Adjust what you plan to spend and save to match your income.
2. Put all of your expenses into categories such as utility bills, rent or mortgage, gasoline, food etc.)
3. Create an envelope for each category
4. Write the amount of money that is to go into that envelope for the month.
5. Each time that you receive money, fill the envelopes accordingly, Keeping track on each envelope.
6. By the end of the month you should have spent the money as planned.

7. Always include an envelope to pay down bills and for savings.

Once I started to use the envelope system, I separated my emotions from my money. I began to feel like I had control over what happened with my money. I started to make my money decisions match my priorities. I you have always wanted to travel yet you never have, you may think that the reason is lack of income. If you use the envelope system, you are likely to find that you have some money to put aside for a future vacation. Start small with a day trip if necessary. No matter what, find the money that you need to do the things that are important to you.

Before I kept track of my money and what I did with it, I would spend it on whatever came up. Over time, what came up was a lot of things that didn't help me in the long run.
Buying fast food was one of the most wasteful things that I did with my money. I consider fast food to be any food that is precooked and ready for me to buy. I consider any food that comes through my car window as not food. Fast-food is a topic in the "baby Momma mentor health" to come.
Fast food is cheap and fast at the moment, but in the long run, it is very costly. I don't know if fast food is addictive, but I do notice that it is habit forming.
The fast food habit is an endless cycle of eating it, not having anything else to eat and eating it again.

I find that the main reason that we eat fast food is because we are starving and we don't have immediate access to anything else to eat. Stop the cycle by creating a weekly menu and buying groceries on a weekly basis.

Create a menu for the week based on your diet and what's on sale at the stores. Buy some ingredients from the local farmer's market.

The higher quality stores do have more expensive items than other stores. Go into these stores with a plan.

Look at the sale papers for all the stores. Know what the store has on sale.

Create envelopes for each of your monthly bills. The lack associated with the baby Momma stigma shows up in the financial resources category. It takes at least two people working, saving and planning to support a child. Unfortunately in many Single Mom situations there is only one person who is financially supportive in the child's life.

Money! Money! Money! Single moms have got to have it! Even if the father is paying child support it is not the same as when two parents are pooling their resources and making financial decisions together. After all, child support is based on the parent's income. As single mothers the amount of money that we spend is not based on our income, it is based on what our children need!

We sacrifice and struggle to make ends meet. No mere check could equal all of the financial work that we do to give our family the lifestyle that it deserves. Even if the mother is the one who is paying the child support she will traditionally earn less money to do the same job as a male counterpart.

Single moms must have the skills to pay the bills. A single mom needs to know what to do with the money once she gets it too.

Either we control our money or the money controls us. Make a plan for your money and you won't have to worry.

Now that you have had your Baby Momma Breakthroughs in the areas of relationships and Anger Management, it is time to manage your money.

Like anger management, money management is a learned skill. Unless someone took the time to teach us great money management skills, we need to learn them now.

Money management is about anticipating income and making plans for it. Money management is about turning the incoming money into whatever you want it to be.

Money management gives you the peace of knowing how much money you made and what you turned that money into.

You can gain the satisfaction of having your bills paid, having a vacation fund or anything else that you want if you priorities your money.

I suggest that you learn the financial techniques that you need. You can find resources in your community to help you if you cannot afford to pay someone to help you. Many churches have financial instruction or stewardship courses. Your local economic development board will offer some help.

We all need to start somewhere to get and keep our financial house in order. I will share the basics of the envelope money management system.

The envelope system in steps:

Create a budget: Write down all your monthly expenses (food, gas bills, hair stylist, clothes etc.) Then write down all of your monthly income. Adjust what you plan to spend and save to match your income.

Put all of your expenses into categories such as utility bills, rent or mortgage, gasoline, food etc.)

Create an envelope for each category

Write the amount of money that is to go into that envelope for the month.

Each time that you receive money, fill the envelopes accordingly, Keeping track on each envelope.

By the end of the month you should have spent the money as planned.

Always include an envelope to pay down bills and for savings.

Once you understand the envelope system you will be ready to move forward.

It is important to save then spend. If you spend then save you will want to save instead of paying bills or buying what you need. Plan ahead for the money to come in and do what you have prioritized for it to do and you will have what you want.

When you manage your money properly you will notice that your income will increase. Whatever we focus on expands and whatever we appreciate, appreciates. If you have a nicely organized place for money to come it will come.

You also need to realize that money is an exchange of energy. Your greatest power and release of energy is in doing what you love. You are good at what you love doing. What you love to do is something that is unique and is your gift to the world. Do more of what you love, take that energy to the places where there is money to exchange for it and have more money.

Don't live your life as a person who believes that money is the root of all evil. No one ever said that. The Bible says in Proverbs that the LOVE of money is the root of all evil.

Money is NOT to be loved. We can love what we do to make money. We love the people who we provide for with money. But don't fall in love with money; that would not be good at all.

Do what you love. Receive income. Manage your money and enjoy your life.

Make more money

In life we do get what we want when we decide to go for it. Go for a better paying job. Pray for the right people to see your talent and accept you into their business.

Work on your people skills. Improve your skills. Network and meet people who will share opportunities with you.

BMB Wisdom: Appreciate your money and it will appreciate.

What we appreciate, appreciates. Give attention to where the money is coming from and where it is going. Use money for what it is for. Pay the bills. Spend it. Keep a healthy flow. Use a budget system to make sure that you have enough money. Start with the envelope system. (A description of the envelope budget system is available for free on my website.)

BMB Wisdom: Have a money mentor.

Do you know how to use money to make more money? Some people do. Learn how to budget and increase your income and invest from a book, a coach, or someone you know. Don't just give them your money; learn how to take care of your money.

BMB Wisdom: Getting organized saves time and Money.

It takes time and sometimes money to organize things. Being organized on a daily basis will keep you from wasting time looking for things and wasting money rebuying things that you can't find.

BMB Wisdom: The secret key to money management is to make more money than you need.

Make more money by learning how you can offer your skills to other people who will pay you. At work make sure you are doing something that is a good fit for you. When you are happy and doing what you love to do you will make more money. One of my favorite jobs was when I was a waitress. The job didn't pay much of a salary. I got more tips than anyone because I loved serving the people.

BMB Wisdom: Have mentors and Mentees

Having a mentor will bring out the best in you. If the person is responsible and has achieved some things that you aspire to achieve they can help you to stay on the right path. They are proof that you can do it. They can also be great references in the future.
Ask someone you admire about how they made it where they are. Be quiet and listen. It can be as simple as a phone conversation once a month.
 Sometimes mentors are people who see potential in you and they begin to help and guide you. I never have asked anyone to be my mentor but I have had many. It just happens over time.
Again we are doing things that are great for us and setting a great example for the kids. If you have a mentor, chances are your child will find mentors throughout their life too.
Mentor someone else too. When you are mentoring someone it always keeps you on your best behavior.

BMB Wisdom: Don't use your kid as an excuse.

If you were a teen mom and you dropped out of High School, don't blame your kids for not graduating. As a matter of fact, finish school if you like. No one wants to feel like they are your excuse.

BMB Wisdom: When something goes wrong, get creative.

Everything happens for a reason. What is done is done. What doesn't kill you makes you stronger. With that said, it's time to creative and move past this.

Other useful phrases include:

How can we fix this? What if we..... Things can still work out if we ...

BMB Wisdom: You have just as much time as everyone else.

You can find the time to do the things that are important to you. I just received an email from a young woman listing all of the reasons that she didn't keep her word. She told me about her classes, her internship etc. She said that she didn't have time to breathe, let alone return my call.
I listened to her quietly because I could relate to what she was saying. I used to make excuses about being busy too. I don't do that anymore.
She simply chose not to call. It wasn't important enough to her to give it her attention. We all have the same amount of time. We choose how we use it.
Just admit that you would rather do something else rather than saying you don't have time.

BMB Wisdom: It's okay for him to be with her.

If your child's father is a good father let him be one. Don't punish him for being with her. It is okay for him to be with her. Somebody has to deal with him on a daily basis. Thank God it's not you. Lol! But seriously, it isn't against the law for them to be together. She can even be around your kid if you two can get to a peaceful place and she is a safe person.

BMB Wisdom: Give what you want to receive.

I believe you reap what you sow; what goes around *does* comes around.

Giving is something that I will always do. When you give from the heart, for the right reasons, you always get more that you give. When I was very young, I used to try to help people and I thought that I ended up getting used. Looking back, I felt used because my help wasn't appreciated or reciprocated.

I soon decided that I would only give when the help would be appreciated. I looked for opportunities to share my natural gifts and talents.

The saying goes, "Give from the saucer and not the cup." In other words give from the overflow. Give naturally. Don't force giving.

BMB Wisdom: A smile goes a long way.

If you don't smile much it is affecting your life. If the problem is your teeth, or what you are thinking, you need to fix it.

New people can decide if they like you or not from across the room. People love a smile.

Your child needs to see you smile. You will get a lot more support and what when you smile too.

BMB Wisdom: Be the hero by finding joy.

During the worst times of my life I always prayed to keep my joyful spirit. I didn't want to become a hardened mean or angry person. I went through many years of sadness and depression but I was always seeking my joy. Today I have found my joy in raising my daughter, writing, coaching, acting, and giving back to others. Finding your joy makes all of the things that we must endure in life worth it. When the final story of your life is told, you are a hero because you eventually found your joy. Win by staying sweet and never getting bitter.

BMB Wisdom: He's the best partner but if he is gone someone else will help.

The child's father is the first choice but if that isn't an option, find another. So many successful people credit their stepfathers, uncles etc.

BMB Wisdom: Celebrate in a healthy way.

I remember my mother splurging to celebrate by buying ice cream or going on a shopping spree. By the end of the celebration, we would be feeling guilty and have a lot less money.
Try to celebrate by doing something fun. Sing a victory song and dance a dance. Buy one thing. Etc.

BMB Wisdom: Don't let your parents ruin your entire life.

Most of my initial consultations include the client mentioning their issues with their parents.

You may have many issues with your parents. If you have children it is time to realize that your children probably have issues with you.

You don't have time to continue to try to figure out what is going on with your parents.

Make a decision about how to do it and move on.

Don't take your parents' behavior personally. Your parents had their personality and beliefs that guided their behavior long before you were born.

BMB Wisdom: Don't use any excuses.

If you want something in your life, don't let anything stop you from going after it. It will never be the perfect time. There will always be something pushing against you trying. Do it now anyway.
You can have results or excuses, not both.

BMB Wisdom: If you think you made a mistake, forgive yourself.

You are responsible for the decisions but not the unpredictable things that happen after. I have had to forgive myself for many things. Unfortunately, hard as I may try, I am not perfect. Sometimes I make mistakes. Some mistakes are harder than others to forgive. Some mothers have big regrets like who their child's father is. No matter how hard you try to forgive the other person, the pain will remain until you forgive yourself.

Trust your gut.
Your head may be afraid but what does the gut say? How does your heart feel about it? Listen to your heart and your gut to make a decision.
Is your child safe? If your gut says no, do something.

BMB Wisdom: Money is not the root of all evil.

I have to make this point because people misquote what is written very often. Money is not the root of evil. People can do evil things but the money isn't doing it

"The love of money is the root of all evil" is written. I agree because if a person falls in love with money, an inanimate object, it is only the beginning of all the evil. As long as you don't fall in love with the paper you can:
Spend money
Make money
Give money
Save money
Invest money
Leave money for loved ones

BMB Wisdom: Laugh every day.

Have you laughed today? Don't be a sour puss. Get your smile on. Watch something funny or call someone who makes you laugh. Think of the last thing that made you laugh.

BMB Wisdom: Turn off the TV.

TV programs are about keeping you sitting down and watching. They call it a boob tube for a reason. It is a nice distraction from time to time. It is nice to help you not think. The key is to remember to turn it off. The United States Surgeon General says limit television to no more than two hours a day. Too much TV is also linked to obesity. Always remember that Television is a business. The purpose isn't to show you the world; it is to make money by keeping you watching. The world that you see on TV isn't necessarily based on reality or helpful in any way. The news will surely give you some remote danger to fear. Increase the love and avoid the sources of fear, like TV.

BMB Wisdom: Soothe your soul.

Try some things such as:
A warm bath
A good movie
Positive music
A talk with a sweet friend
A professional or loving massage
Writing in a gratitude journal
Aromatherapy with essential oils
Hugging your pet
Hugging your child
Watching sunset
Prayer
Meditation
Sing along with your favorite happy song.
Dance around
Put on something sexy and pose in the mirror
Try some of the above things. You may feel better than if you had taken a drink.

BMB Wisdom: Keep on Dancing.

Play the music you love and move the way you want to move. Dancing is fun exercise and if no one is watching except maybe your child, let loose.

Turn on the music.
Turn on some music and keep moving.

BMB Wisdom: You are not a victim.

Remember, "Your story doesn't define you. You can defy your story."

You may have been through it all in the past but you are not a victim. You are a wonderful person with the most precious gift called life. You are a powerful creator. Things happen so that you may overcome them, learn from them and help yourself and others. You have the power.

BMB Wisdom: Everything happens for a reason.

We don't always see why looking forward, but when we look back, we will see that everything happens for a reason. When something unexpected happens just know that there is some unknown reason. Just roll with it.

BMB Wisdom: Be honest.

This way you won't have any lies to remember. You will sleep well. You don't have to live a lie.

BMB Wisdom: Get out of negative energy environments

I know the joy of leaving turmoil. I left my family's house and ran away at age 12 because the environment was toxic for me.

I found peace in other situations. If you have daily conflict in your home, find a way out. If your neighborhood is unsafe, find a way to live somewhere else. When you move, leave the negativity behind. Don't take arguments, yelling, etc. with you to a new situation.

BMB Wisdom: Use your shower time to imagine cleaning off all negativity.

Everything is energy. Negative energy can be around us when we go outside every day. Energy is like the way that you can "Feel" someone looking at you. You feel the energy that is coming your way. Negative energy can affect you and make you feel tired or negative yourself. Take a shower and imagine all of the energy from other people getting rinsed off and flowing down the drain.

BMB Wisdom: Take things one thing at a time.

"A woman's work is never done."
This quote is still true as I write these words. There is always something else to be done. I can easily get depressed or overwhelmed when I start getting ahead of myself. I am only one person and it is good enough for me to do things one at a time.
I used to help with the homework while doing my hair, while calling the gas company and cooking dinner. It is too much. Put things in order of priority and give your attention to one thing at a time if possible. Put quality over quantity.

BMB Wisdom: Do what you love as often as possible.

I have friends and clients who tell me, I used to love to … I always think to myself and eventually ask them "Why did you stop doing it?"
The answer is typically "I did that before I had my child."
If you love something do it if you can. The things that you love to do are a part of you. These things are part of what you live to do. Do these things if they are healthy and safe enough. Let your child see the joy that you have when you do these things. There is a chance that they won't understand why you love to do what you love to do. It will help them just to see how wonderful an activity can be for you. This will help them to appreciate the things that make them happy.

BMB Wisdom: Make progress over the years.

No, not one of us is perfect. You can get better. I try to get better each day. It is important to improve because things get easier and life becomes your masterpiece. Our kids are growing and learning so we need to set a good example and be growing and learning too. Ever see an elderly person who is full of life? It makes you feel good. If you see an elderly person who is just sitting there without any interaction with the world it makes you sad. Be uplifting to yourself and your family by staying active mentally and physically as you get older.

BMB Wisdom: Try new things just for trying's sake.

Try it, you may like it.
New food
 New genre of books
New type of friends
 New hobby
Try it.

BMB Wisdom: Worrying is optional and unnecessary.

What you spend most of your time thinking about is what you will see. Have you ever started thinking about a certain car? All of a sudden you see that car everywhere. Problems are like that too. Think of a certain problem and you can start to see it everywhere too. Asking questions in your mind like, "What will I do if I lose my job" or "How would I live if…" this or that happened are questions that lead your curiosity in a direction that you do not want to go in. instead think things like, "Things always work out." Or "No matter what happens I will be okay." Even if the worst happens, you will make it best. Expect the best and handle what happens.

BMB Wisdom: Don't compare the way your life feels to the way that other people's looks.

I think that Serena Williams has a great life. She is a champion. She is known for her beauty. She is rich. She dates extremely wealthy me. From my point of view, she is living a wow life. I don't think her life is any better than mine because my life is wow too. My life is a miracle. My life is mine. Serena's life is hers. I appreciate the inspiration, entertainment and joy that her life has brought to mine. However, I am still happy to be me and not her. While she was practicing tennis, I was living my life lessons that I am writing in this book.

Rap artist J.Cole has a song that says "There is no life better than yours." I agree. I love this song because I know that this is true. You can sit and look at what other people have and wish that you had it too, or you can appreciate what you have and enjoy it. Why waste your life wanting someone else's. They may be looking at you and seeing all the greatness of your life. If you want a better relationship, car, job, house, vacation etc. realized that none of those things can make you enjoy your life. Enjoy your life now. If you want more take steps to get it, but enjoy your life now.

BMB Wisdom: Tell your loved ones that you love them.

I know a few people who lost loved ones and they regret not telling them that they love them before they passed away. Also there is a saying that "People don't care what you know until they know that you care." Let people know that you care.

BMB Wisdom: Look at the highlight reel of your day and life.

Look back on the day and see everything that you accomplished. See your successes. This is a good way to stop negative thoughts. When the negative thoughts start, start watching your highlight reel. Remember walking across the stage in High School or the day your hair, nails, dress, shoes and makeup were flawless. See the good things that you have done today to keep the negative thoughts away. Think positively about you.

BMB Wisdom: Feel the fear and act anyway.

Fear is what will trick you if you let it. Fear will say "but what if something goes wrong?" The key is to take the risk so that something can go right. Overcome the fear. Do the scary thing that you know **will be good for you**. Expect things to go righter than they ever have before.

BMB Wisdom: Let your haters help you.

I have had haters since elementary school. One particular bully was obsessed with me from second grade to high school. I say obsessed with me because she was. She always noticed my hair and my clothes and what I was doing. She would notice when I was absent. She made terrible comments to me and hurt my feelings regularly, but looking back, she gave me more attention than my own family. She was correct about my weaknesses too. I was socially awkward and a follower. It doesn't bother me now because I made it through that time and I am no longer a victim.

I don't fear haters or bullies. They have nothing better to do than analyze me and give me feedback. I don't go looking for them but I am not afraid of them either. Every now and then I get that comment or that look. I think about my old school bully. If the comment doesn't apply I let it fly away and forget it. If it is something that I want to improve, it reminds me that I can.

BMB Wisdom: Have a vision.

Like a plant, things either grow or die. Your vision is you growth guide. Having a vision is giving yourself and your team a motivation to get up every day. The vision is who you are becoming more and more each day. Write the vision and visualize it every day. Whatever your vision, I believe that one day you will be living it out.

Use a vision board. A vision board is a display of pictures and words that you have chosen to represent things that you are attracting into your life. Many successful people have created vision boards. I am a Certified Vision Board Coach. There are some guidelines so I suggest that you seek some guidance in creating your vision board. I am currently creating videos for my YouTube channel that will give some guidelines. You can check tanyatalley.com for more information.

Vision Boards are fun to make. Soon you will see everything that you put on your vision board enter your real life.

Have a vision for your family.

It is written that people perish for lack of vision. If you don't know where you are going then you can end up anywhere at any time. Where is your family headed? Hopefully your family is headed to fulfilling your positive vision for the future.

BMB Wisdom: Create Your Own Bliss

Create the environment that you love. Do whatever it takes to get out of a bad neighborhood. Your child needs to attend a better school. Love the people who surround you. In your own mind and heart fill your surroundings with love.
The choice is always yours.

> One day you will have the blessing to share with someone else that this is how you overcame the baby momma stigma. This is how you became a successful single mom. This is how you found your bliss.

Breakthrough Success for Single Mothers

No one will ever **give** you your dream or your success. You have to go for it!

We all have a power within. We will have what we focus on.

If we know what we want, and believe in it with feeling, we will have it.

Think about what you like.

Soon you will like your life more and more. Your life will become an obvious success.

You will get out of the baby momma survival mode. You will find your **B.L.I.S.S.**

You are so much more than a label or a situation. You are a creator of a beautiful life.

When I met Tiffany she was bogged down with negative feelings in a negative situation.

Today Tiffany has created a much better life for herself. She reclaimed her youth.

Once Tiffany used the Steps in this book she was free to create whatever she wanted her life to be day by day.

She wanted a great relationship. Her new dating skills paid off and she met a wonderful man. She is happy in a healthy long term relationship.

Tiffany started a small school near her house. Her business is making good money and she knows that she is helping the families in her neighborhood. The changes that Tiffany made have changed her entire neighborhood.

Her man is her companion, confidant, lover and protector. Her child is happy and well adjusted. This is what she wanted, this is what she created and this is what she has now.

Write down what you want in detail. Close your eyes and feel what having that feels like; hear it, smell it, taste it, touch it, say it.

When you open your eyes stay on the path
Knowing what you want, talking about what you want and having what you want is your new hobby. In your unified home, with healthy relationships, your anger and your money is managed. You are an example of happiness for your child. You have the blessings of bliss.

Soon you will be surrounded by what you love. You will soon be doing what you want to do with the people you want to do them with; you bliss will be contagious.

You will know in your heart that you are a single mom success and so will your child.

As for me I am blissfully satisfied with my life. I am overjoyed that I am giving myself my best possible life. I believe that my daughter is much happier because she I am happy. I believe that she is improving miraculously because she is happy.

Destiny is connected to her inner B.L.I.S.S. and I feel that I am doing my job as her mother.

Life is good one moment at a time. Every moment, choose bliss.
Bliss is always available to you from within.

Thank You!

You are part of my dream now. Thank you for taking the step of picking up this book and reading it.
 I appreciate you.
Please use the contact information in the *About the Author* section of this book to contact me.
Let me know what your goals and dreams are and how this book has affected you.
If you are taking the journey to find your B.L.I.S.S., reach out so that I can believe in your success with you.

 Blessings of love and bliss,

Tanya

Acknowledgments

Although I wrote, edited and published this book by myself, I want to thank the following people for having a positive impact on my life and for helping me along my path in life. I left home at an early age and some of you kept me safe. I needed lots of love to heal and some of you loved me beyond my imagination. Some of you gave me encouraging words that nourished my soul.

Thank you. I love you all.

- Adrienne Paige-Thank you for being an angel to me.
- Florence Bagsby DTM
- Mary Kane-My sister and first best friend
- Deborah Talley-thank you for giving me books
- Ronald Talley-thank you for the coaching spirit
- Regina Rhymes, DTM
- Leslie Pogue
- Jacqueline "Jackie" Jones (Lucien)
- Nina "Dr. Neen" Craft
- Dr. Joyce Craft
- Chet Craft
- Albert Yang
- Evelyn Woolridge DTM
- Mine Lenoir
- Toastwriters Toastmasters Club in Santa Monica, CA
- TopSales Toastmasters Club 3032555
- Michael Genzuk of USC
- Lyrice
- Ella Mae Brown
- Luana Garrison

- Alycia Moore from MIP
- Denise at Umeworks.com -web designer
- Cynthia Lamb
- Reyhan Sun
- Erika Williams
- Trish Stewart-Makeup Artist and Beauty Consultant
- Shay Win
- Marcus Tyrone-Motivational Speaker
- Esat Sun
- Dale Hughes
- Tany Sousanna-PR Maven
- Judy Blume-thank you for writing books that were my best friends growing up.

Endnotes

*Selected worksheets mentioned are available for download tanyatalley.com

+No character depicted in this book is intended to represent any actual individual who is living or deceased.

Single Mom Statistics
http://singleparents.about.com/od/legalissues/p/portrait.htm
 http://www.census.gov/prod/2009pubs/p60-237.pdf
http://www.census.gov/prod/2011pubs/p60-240.pdf
Footnotes
***Journal of Personality and Social Psychology 84 (2:) 365-376 See also www.wikipedia.org/ Psychological resilience

About the Author

Bliss Breakthrough Success Facilitator Tanya Talley has helped many women reach their dreams of starting a business, changing careers, overcoming past issues and more.

Tanya provides coaching and workshops that promote personal development through goal setting, anger management, budgeting, and Emotional healing to create a more B.L.I.S.S.ful life.

Tanya is a certified Master of Neuro-Linguistic Programming (NLP), Emotional Freedom Techniques (EFT), Hypnosis as well as Certified Vision Board Coach.

Upcoming books include: "Relationship Bliss Breakthrough" "My L.A.U.S.D. Education" & "Cerulea"

Contact Tanya today to
- Share your story
- Give feedback about this book
- Book her as a speaker
- To organize/participate in a Single Mom Success/Personal Development workshop
- To receive worksheets on any Baby Momma Bliss topic.

tanyatalley.com
Email: tanya@tanyatalley.com